Mom Did SO Put Me in Charge
Running the World as a Middle Child

Written by Jonnie Garstka
Illustrated by Charlotte K. Schwartz

Mom Did SO Put Me in Charge is a collection of the author's memories and recollections. It is all true...unless you ask her family....

Copyright© 2024 by Jonnie Garstka

All rights reserved.

Published in the United States by Riverhaven Books, Massachusetts.

ISBN: 978-1-951854-41-6

Printed in the United States of America
by Country Press, Lakeville, Massachusetts

Edited by Riverhaven Books
Designed by Stephanie Lynn Blackman
Whitman, MA

TO DEDICATE OR NOT TO DEDICATE, THAT IS THE QUESTION

I have written three books,
each of which is a collection of my newspaper columns.
The first, *I Started Out as A Middle Child*,
I dedicated to my sister Sandie who died of
a heart attack when she was in her early sixties.
To Sandie, "When you left us, Gret became the sole middle child,
instead of a collective one with me. Now she'd being a pain.
Isn't there something you can do about this?"

****

The second, *You're Not the Boss of Me*,
I dedicated to my brother Joe who died of
Alzheimer's Disease.
To Joe, "You were the best oldest brother ever,
even if you did paint my nose."

****

The third, *Mom Did So Put Me in Charge*, is dedicated to
my brother Moe, who died
last year of cancer.
To Moe, "You always said you were Mom's favorite.
Now you can ask her.
If you made
it to heaven, that is."

It's funny, my six remaining siblings think I should stop writing books, or at the very least, dedicate any future ones to other people.

Imagine.

Table of Contents

The Middle Child – That Would Be Me 1
    Branching Out 3
    Elizabeth Is A Stupid Name 4
    To See With The Eyes Of A Child 6
    Erin Go Bragh 7
    A Lisping Letter From Me 8
    Shouldn't I Get Credit For Biting My Tongue? 9
    "How Do I Love Thee? Let Me Count The Ways." 10
    Open Mouth, Insert Foot 11
    For Priscilla 12
    How To Get A Bionic Knee In Six Easy Steps 13
    For Sara 14
    The "Me" Nobody Knows 15
    Magister Dixit 16
    Zen Things 18
    My Grownup Best Friend 20
    A School Bus, A Kindergartener, And A Man With Tattoos 22
    Grandma's Recipe For Happiness 23
    Fun With Words 24
    When? 26
    Our Holiday Get Together 27
    "Good Fences Make Good Neighbors" ~Robert Frost 28
    Bathroom Grafitti 29
    How Mature Adults Argue 30
    "A Rose By Any Other Name . . ." 32
    Someone Who Shows Up 34
    Comfort Food? I Think Not. 35
    My Amazing Gardening Skills 36

What Papa Said	38
Why I Don't Allow Guns In Our House	39
Check The Oil	40
Annoying? Moi?	42
What I Did On My Spring Vacation	44
The Things We Do For Love	46
My Winter Adventure	47
You're Not The Boss Of Me	48
Finding My Voice Again	49
No Place Like Home	50
Don't Let The Door Hit Ya On The Way Out	51
Parents: How To Raise Them	**52**
Your Eyes Are Bigger Than Your Stomach	53
Mom Stories, We All Tell Them	54
How Not To Manage Money	56
The Church And Mom And Me	57
The Sixth Sense	59
Mr. Oliver And Our Mom	61
Siblings: How Many Is Too Many?	**62**
"There Is Only One Thing More Precious Than Time, And That's Who We Spend It With."	63
For Those We Loved And Lost…	64
My Two Older Brothers	65
Family Is Everything	66
For My Brothers, I Love You	68
Turns Out We Did Walk Uphill Both Ways	69
Sibling Time Together	71
My Tribe	73
Family Food Stories	75

Did They Really Say That?	77
My 'Safe Place' Is A Table	79
Holiday Crazies	81
Laisse Faire	82
Dolls I Have Known	83
"I Wish I Grew Up In The Same Family You Did."	85
Brothers Aren't So Bad	86
Mom's Ring	87
When I Was A Camel	88
Chris's Birthday	89
"Alas For Those Who Never Sing But Die With All Their Music In Them."	91
Just Jonnie	92
Pat's Shampoo	93
Our Kids, Practically Perfect	**94**
"Have Your Child Bring A Sweater"	95
A Kindergartener And A First Grader Walk Onto A Playground	97
When The Going Gets Tough, Lower Your Standards	98
Paul's Good Report Card	100
A Mother's Gift	102
How To Spoil Your Grandchildren	104
"These Are The Times That Try Men's Souls."	106
Daughters' Day	108
Our Pets – Each One Almost A Purebred	**109**
The Vet Said What?	110
Choices	111
"Don't Cry Because It's Over. Smile Because It Happenened."	113
Another Member Of The Family	114
Sophie Becomes A Woman . . .	115

Sophie, The Music Critic	117
How Max, Gretchen's Dog, Taught Me A Lesson	118
A Doggy Vocabulary Lesson	119
My Opinion, Which Is Always Right	120
Let Me Tell You A Story . . .	121
A New Fourth Of July Tradition	124
Angels Among Us	125
"Cowards Die Many Times. The Valiant Taste Of Death But Once."	126
To Believe Or Not To Believe, That Is The Question	127
An Important Letter To My Family	129
I Remember Marji	130
Funeral Stories	131

The Middle Child – That Would Be Me

BRANCHING OUT

Mom called it "disappearing." She said she didn't mind if I disappeared, as long as I did my chores before I vanished.

My secret hideout was an apple tree. I would climb it, bring one or two books and a bottle of juice, and read to my heart's content.

The straight part of our driveway was 180 feet long. When it came within a car's length of the front lawn, it turned right and then circled the entire area around the house. My favorite tree was outside the circle, and as such, didn't get much attention.

As you may well know, apple trees are pruned to stay low to the ground. This makes harvesting their fruit much easier. This also makes a fall out of the tree not too bad. Not that I'm admitting that I ever did fall, I'm just explaining things. But if I were to fall again, I wouldn't try so hard to protect a stupid library book.

Mom understood that sometimes I wanted to get away from "The Madding Crowd." I think she "got" me, because she too would have liked a few hours of peace and quiet away from our own "Madding Crowd," the eight kids still living at home.

One time she told me I was in the larva phase of my life, and that the pupa stage was just around the corner. I looked this up in our encyclopedia and thought it sounded neat.

I went back to Mom and asked her if she thought I was an insect because I "bugged" her. We laughed together. Then I went back to my tree.

Jane Eyre was calling.

ELIZABETH IS A STUPID NAME

Every once in a while, I get a picture of what my poor teachers had to deal with when I was in their classes. I went to parochial schools for sixteen years, and I now wonder just how many of the good sisters I sent to the Happy Home for Crazed Nuns. That I thought the Little Flower, Saint Theresa, was a boring saint should have been punishment enough for my fourth-grade teacher. But, when I think about my talking a few of my pals into voting for Joan of Arc, because I assured them burning at the steak combined dinner and sainthood, I wince.

Be that as it may, let's talk about the sacrament of Confirmation. My name was "Joan Mary Lane," possibly the most boring name ever. When a Catholic girl gets confirmed, she has the honor of choosing a saint's name to add to her own; the thought being that the saint would guide the burgeoning Christian on her life's path.

I was jubilant! I was going to find a really cool saint's name. Then "Joan Lane" plus an amazing saint's name would be remembered with awe and respect.

I studied and checked out a truck load of saints. My teacher was gratified by my renewed religious zeal. On a nightly basis, as we worked on dinner, doing things like peeling carrots and potatoes, I would regale my mom with my searches and possible choices.

Saint Francis was okay, but he was a gentle person, and "Joan Mary Francis" didn't have the panache I was looking for.

Saint Paul was cool. After all he did get struck by lightning, but Paul was my brother Moe's real name . . .

This went on for a while until I came upon Saint Wenceslaus. Now, that was a great name! "Joan Mary Wenceslaus," yup, that would be my choice. I was going to rock the ceremony when the bishop said my saint's name.

A part of the ritual of the sacrament of Confirmation is a slap on the face. The good nuns assured us it was a symbolic gesture to show us that now that we were adults in the eyes of the church, we should be willing to suffer for our faith. A few of us were disappointed that it wasn't going to be a real slap, because we knew which kids would be upset, but I digress.

Confirmation day dawned. The bishop looked regal and we, the candidates, were dressed in our Sunday best. I believe the hope was that we would behave if we were wearing our good clothing.

When the bishop came to me, he said, "Joan Mary Elizabeth." I protested. "But Bishop," said I. "My saint's name is supposed to be Wenceslaus . . ."

He cracked my face so hard my head turned around. I managed to croak "Okay, Elizabeth it is . . ." But he had already moved along the line of candidates, and was gently tapping Carol Ann Kolkmeyer's sweet face.

Betrayed, I was inconsolable. Somebody changed my name choice, and I had a bishop's palm print on the left side of my face. I asked my mom. "How am I going to stand out in the world with a name like Elizabeth?"

She reassured me it would happen someday, but that it just might take a while.

Then we went out for ice cream and everything was better.

Signed,
Joan Mary Wenceslaus Lane Garstka

P.S. Elizabeth is still a stupid name

TO SEE WITH THE EYES OF A CHILD

I was our town's Easter Bunny for three years. In full rabbit regalia, I gave out treats and hugs, and posed for pictures at our annual Easter Egg Hunt.

One year, I picked up my costume a few days early. My bestie and I called the local elementary school to ask if we could visit? And, with their blessing, we did.

Some of the older children questioned whether or not I was the "REAL" Easter Bunny…

I felt a small hand patting my costumed behind. Then a little girl appeared at my side, shouting, "It's the Easter Bunny all right. I checked his butt, and he has a fluffy tail and everything.

Reassured, the nonbelievers then allowed me to continue to give out jellybean treats.

Who would have thought the testimonial of a blind little girl affirming that I had a "fluffy tail," would convince the other kids that I was real?

The Easter Bunny wept a little that day.

ERIN GO BRAGH

Peg was an elderly Irish woman who lived in our apartment complex. She was warm and witty and a sort of surrogate mother for many of us. One autumn day we both happened to be at the trash area at the same time. As we both tossed our bags into the dumpster, she said, "You're having a girl. How lovely."

As I was hugely pregnant, I wasn't surprised that she knew this. It was her absolute confidence that I was going to have a girl that rattled me.

Paul and I did not know the gender of this, our second child, but I voiced my appreciation for her kind words, and hoped.

It was a girl! Gretchen arrived that October with the requisite ten fingers and toes and a smile that turned her dad into silly putty.

Fast forward two years, and I again ran across Peg at the recycle/dumpster site. Busy with my young family, I hadn't seen her for months. She said, "Are you and Paul happy that you're having another girl?"

Another girl? I didn't even know I was pregnant!

I truly thought Peg was "fey." (The Irish believe this means one has "the sight.")

Because, as it turned out, her predictions were correct both times; times in which I had not known enough to have given her clues.

The next time I saw her, months later, I asked Peg outright, "How did you know I was having a girl when I didn't even know I was pregnant? Are you fey?"

She looked surprised, as if it all should have been as obvious to me, as it was to her. "No, of course not. I'm not fey at all. Both times, Dear, you totally lost your looks. Everyone knows, if the babe in the uterus is a girl, she steals her mother's beauty."

A LISPING LETTER FROM ME

Dear Everyone,

I had oral surgery this week. I'm fine but seem to be writing the same way I'm talking, (and looking) which is odd. I'm not going out for a bit as the Paparazzi love to catch us major stars in awkward situations and, as we all know, my face is my fortune.

Sophie, the pup, looked at my swollen jaw and ran the other way, her tail between her legs.

Paul's reaction was pretty much the same.

Oh, I'll be back, better than ever. Well, better. It just may take a while.

Know I love you all and will have a nice smile soon.

Not soon enough for me, but soon.

SHOULDN'T I GET CREDIT FOR BITING MY TONGUE?

When the dentist said, "You should have a crown," I snorted, nodded my head, and said, "I know. I know."

Seriously, I lost a crown two months ago, had oral surgery, and am now waiting to heal enough to get a new one. Before the operation, I asked the surgeon if I would have any dietary restrictions.

He cheerfully said, "No, just chew on the other side of your mouth."

I had been thinking I might lose a few pounds having to be cautious, and possibly, dealing with pain. Nope, I powered on through and managed to consume my normal quantities of food, albeit more slowly and carefully. Actually, I have gnawed on the inside of my mouth too many times to count. I am also "biting my tongue" on a daily basis, which is something I'm not known to do.

My friends are starting to think I've matured and become a kinder, gentler person…

This whole experience has made me more aware of others who have or have had dental issues. I find myself being nice to them.

This is a big step for me.

"HOW DO I LOVE THEE? LET ME COUNT THE WAYS."
~Elizabeth Barrett Browning

What I've missed most during this time of quarantine, has been the ability to physically touch the ones I love. I've been truly lucky to have Paul sequestered with me, for I know there are many, at this time, who are completely alone. I guess I'm surprised by the depth of my longing to be with my family.

All of our adult children are working from home. The last thing they need is a visit from Paul and me, two amazing, brilliant and, good looking, senior citizens. We would only be something more for them to worry about. So no grandchild hugging can happen for a while.

Years ago, during flu season, our parish suspended its custom of extending and giving the "Handshake of Peace." They were concerned about us possibly passing germs to one another. On the way home after Mass, that first Sunday, Paul said. "That was sad."

I looked askance at him, so he continued.

"I bet for some of the older parishioners the sign of peace is the only physical, human contact they have all week."

He was right. While I had been, unselfishly, thinking about bacon and eggs and scones for breakfast, he had been thinking of others.

Elbow bumping, saluting, waving, winking, etc. will have to do us for a while. Sadly, a mask, while protecting us, also hides the smiles we instinctively give to our children, their children, and our friends.

I know we will return from this pandemic, stronger, and, hopefully, wiser. But for now, let's follow the rules.

(I ask those of you who know my siblings to ignore their snidely remarks about me and rule following. First, I didn't know I wasn't supposed to run across the Merritt Parkway. Besides, doing that cut my mile walk to school in half. Second, I was in Kindergarten. How was I supposed to know it was against the rules?)

OPEN MOUTH, INSERT FOOT

It was 90 degrees outside and humid as all get out. Paul came into the kitchen and could not believe I was baking cookies. He made mention of our extremely hardworking air conditioning system and left the room, shaking his head.

I didn't have a good reason to defend the idiocy of my having the oven set at 375 degrees. I just felt guilty.

My neighbors' grandkids were leaving the next day to visit their father, who lives in another state. The children didn't seem thrilled at the thought of spending a month away.

Their stepdad Bill, who was driving the kids somewhere, saw me walking Miss Sophie, and stopped to chat. That was when he told me their father lived in Ohio.

I opened my (big) mouth to say that when my parents moved to Ohio, I had a serious problem with the people there...

Bill asked me what the problem was. (Rolling his eyes backward to indicate the two avidly listening children)

I said, "The people there are kind, and, well, nice." I continued to noisily complain that my sarcastic, amazing, New England sense of humor was wasted on genuine, thoughtful people.

When Bill remarked that the kids would be flying to Ohio the following day, I felt I owed the children something for my "problem with the people of Ohio" gaffe. So, I asked them if they would need some cookies for the plane ride? They laughed and said, "Yes."

That is why, on a humid, 90-degree day, I baked cookies for two darling children and their dad, who lives in Ohio.

FOR PRISCILLA

I did a nice thing for my friend last week. I drove her into my favorite city, Boston.

You would think I gave her a kidney.

She insisted on paying for my breakfast, for valet parking, and would have filled the car's gas tank if it hadn't already been full. She also prepared a meal for Paul and me, as I would have been too busy waiting for her to make dinner that night. And the last straw? She gave me a gift and an amazing letter, telling me how wonderful I am.

She is as close to me as a sister. Doesn't she get that I would give her a kidney if she needed one? There may be more trips to Mass General in our future, so I have to nip this grateful attitude in the bud. I love Boston, and I love her. However, if she keeps this up, I'm going to have to do to her what I used to do to any one of my five sisters when she annoyed me:

1. Smack her upside the head (a la Gibbs in NCIS)
2. Short sheet her bed
3. Put salt in the sugar bowl
4. Wear her favorite blouse and look better in it than she does
5. Read her diary aloud, with the appropriate pathos in my voice
6. Borrow her car and return it with an empty gas tank

These should straighten her out, right?

If not, then I'll have to get really tough and do to her what I used to do to any one of my four brothers when they annoyed me. She probably doesn't wear a jock strap though.

Too bad.

HOW TO GET A BIONIC KNEE IN SIX EASY STEPS

When next you read this, I will be the proud owner of my second bionic knee. Those of us who have had this fun experience know one does not make the decision to do this casually. For three years, Covid saved my cowardly, sorry ass by making me postpone the surgery. But then, when I realized my elderly dog, Bridget, was walking slower for me, rather than the other way around, I had to put my big girl pants on and set this up.

A bunch of tests and criteria had to be met in the course of this adventure. When the Physician's Assistant said, "No alcohol for a week before the surgery." I was pretty sure she meant a work week, which is, as we all know, five days, not seven.

Health Care Proxy? I didn't remember them requiring one last time, so I asked, "Are you guys trying to tell me something?"

Then there was the antibiotic body wash I had to shower with for three days. (Paul really liked its Clorox-like fragrance.) After the phlebotomist drew two vials of blood, she used a cotton ball and masking tape to bandage my inner elbow. When I asked her for a Hello Kitty band-aid, she said she didn't have any. And they call themselves professionals!

They took preparatory X-rays of my knees and hips. When I asked why the hips, the young technician explained that sometimes there is a hip anomaly that might have compounded the knee issue. This made sense to me. Later, when I was in the surgeon's office, he showed me the X-rays.

When I looked at the hip ones, I thought, "Paul says I'm a tight ass. That ass doesn't look tight to me."

When I looked back at the doctor, his face was in his hands.

Mortified, I asked him. "I didn't say that out loud, did I?" He just nodded.

Then, for me, the final humiliation came when I had to get on a scale. The reading was in kilograms, which convert to weirder numbers than pounds do. I nearly fainted when I saw my number. The nurse tried to calm me down, asking did I want to know my weight in pounds?

When I said, "Hell no!" she laughed. I liked her.

So, Dear Ones, when next you see me, I will be sporting a brand-new reason to be X-rayed and patted down every time I travel.

FOR SARA

This Saturday Paul and I will be attending the wedding of our neighbors' darling daughter.

Since we are at the sad age where we attend more memorials than weddings, I've been having fun getting ready. I bought some new clothes, changed my hair appointment to closer to the big day, got a mani-pedi yesterday, and have had two self-inflicted facials.

Sophie, our puppy, and I have added mileage to our walks in the futile hope I would somehow not only regain the amazing body of my youth but also strengthen my ten-month old new knee so I can perform my amazing signature dance moves.

I asked my granddaughter to help me with makeup, as I seldom wear much. I was beginning to feel sorry for the bride as, clearly, I was going to outshine her on her big day.

Last night when I was horsing around with Sophie, she head-butted me. I thought she might have broken my nose, but quickly got out, and applied, my miracle remedy, frozen peas, and thought all would be well on the morrow. And today, my nose is fine. I do, however, have a pretty impressive shiner.

I had been prepared to be really clever, as well as terrific looking, on "The Big Day." The line I had been planning to put in their "book of wisdom from older couples" was, "Forget about never going to bed angry with each other, you will." But in light of my black eye, it is no longer funny.

In a way, I'm glad I won't be the best-looking person at the wedding.

It should be the bride.

THE "ME" NOBODY KNOWS

I don't think I ever thought about the difference between crying and weeping until now. That I never cry has always been something of a source of pride for me.

That I've had two broken legs, two broken thumbs (baseball), two broken pinkies (softball), two knee replacements, cancer, and more than twenty stitches on this amazing face, with not a single tear shed, is normal for me.

However, I do get verklempt over phone commercial featuring a dad and his daughter. I get teary over my kids' and grandkids' milestones, first words, first steps, first loves, etc. And when I had to put down beloved pets, our old dogs, our baby kittens, I was a mess.

Ironically, I was always the stoic when our children were injured. Why? Because Paul always fell apart when the injuries occurred. Having been an only child, Paul had never seen injuries like Jim's stitches, Gretchen's broken leg, or Steph's concussions. They were all "firsts" for him.

I would hazard the guess that my seeing similar injuries in my family, and knowing they had not been life threatening, gave me an edge in those situations.

Additionally, crying at those times would not have helped the injured party/child/sibling.

Be that as it may, my being upset over pain others are dealing with happens more often than I care to admit.

So "The Me Nobody Knows" is a card-carrying crybaby who weeps often for others, just not for herself when she breaks her own leg, cuts her own hand, or gives herself another black eye walking into the cupboard door she just opened.

I do, however, say many, many bad words when these injuries happen. But they don't count as crying, right?

MAGISTER DIXIT

I was always going to be a teacher. As a youngster I used to line up our dogs, cats, and whichever younger siblings were still afraid of me for pretend school.

There would be nursery rhymes to be recited, the "ABCD" song to be sung, and snacks for everyone who stayed for the whole lesson.

The dogs were always good. The cats, not so much. Chris, Pat, and Mike's attendance depended on the kind of cookies served at the end of class.

Five of the ten of us became teachers. Chris has a PhD in computers, Joe and Puss have Masters' Degrees (Puss said her preadolescent psychology work was a boon when she worked in a 'Good Old Boys' Bank in Georgia), Gret has always worked with special needs children. She still volunteers despite being "retired." My captive audiences were middle school and high school kids.

Sometimes our dad would POO-POO teaching as a profession. Our mom would then remind him that someone taught Beethoven how to play the piano, someone put a paint brush in Picasso's hand, and someone taught Marie Curie chemistry.

I loved teaching. The kids' personalities seemed to shine through the teen perils of braces, acne, bad hair days, and ill-fitting clothing due to irregular growth spurts.

I always felt I learned as much from my kids as I taught them, usually more. One of my favorite lessons was what I called "THE ME NOBODY KNOWS."

I had worked copious hours on another project that failed dismally the first time I introduced it.

On a wing and a prayer, I tossed out the idea of "THE ME NOBODY KNOWS," and the kids embraced it. It involved them talking about their favorite book, song, movie, nursery rhyme, and hobby. They each then made a poster that celebrated all of the above, visually celebrating their unique selves.

I'll never forget the kids' stunned reaction when the "class clown" explained that he took care of his younger siblings (his nursery rhyme segment) after school, when his mom went to chemo.

Teaching was often difficult. Young lives aren't always full of fun, and teenagers can be powder kegs of raw emotion. But the hard times, the angry confrontations, and the ugly tears (mine) made the good days shine.

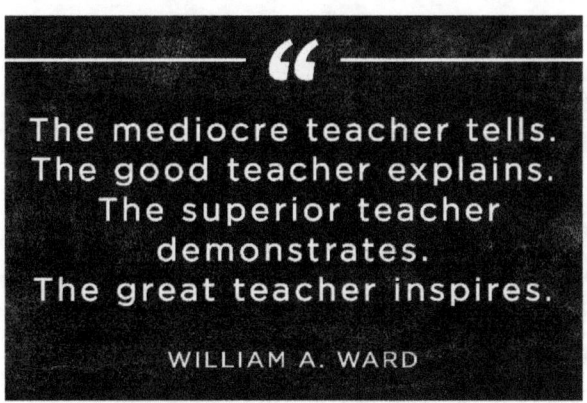

"
The mediocre teacher tells.
The good teacher explains.
The superior teacher demonstrates.
The great teacher inspires.

WILLIAM A. WARD

ZEN THINGS

It's my turn to share a lesson about writing with my writing circle pals. We often use learning components to help hone our skills, and we take turns giving the talks.

Since we have been meeting for ten years, we've actually covered just about every writerly topic from grammar to characterization, dialogue to suspense, opening sentences to closing sentences to conflict to credibility, etc., etc.

Happily, as seniors, we've probably forgotten half of the lessons we've been taught, so I should be home free with whichever skill I choose. While looking for ideas in some of my old magazines, I came upon a list of what were called "Zen things" and knew I had a winner.

I'm sharing these with you now because they can be applied to any goal in life we wish to accomplish. And, because it's a new year…

- ☐ Do one thing at a time.
- ☐ Do it slowly and deliberately.
- ☐ Do it completely.
- ☐ Do less.
- ☐ Put space between things.
- ☐ Develop rituals.
- ☐ Designate time for certain things.
- ☐ Devote time to sitting.
- ☐ Smile and serve others.
- ☐ Make cleaning and cooking become meditation.
- ☐ Think about what is necessary.
- ☐ Live simply

I've been working on 'doing one thing at a time.'

"Why?" You ask.

Because I have the bad habit of trying to multitask, and not doing it well. Witness last week when I put our holiday decorations back in the attic and locked Sam, our cat, and Sophie, our dog, in there too.

Another good 'one thing at a time' thing I should do might be to have clothes on when I answer the front door. My neighbor seemed to like my flannel pjs, but Paul was not amused.

    I offer these 'Zen things' to help you to begin this new year renewed, and to protect your pets and small grandchildren from attic incarcerations.

MY GROWNUP BEST FRIEND

I think we all remember the 'best friend' we had in high school. Mine was smart and funny and, for lack of a better word, "alive." She took no prisoners but was a pile of mush over injured animals and timid freshmen. We lost touch in the years since our halcyon days. But when I think of her, I smile.

When we moved to Plymouth ten years ago, I knew it was the beginning of the next phase of Paul's and my lives. Unfairly, I know now, I had little hope of finding a female soulmate, someone who would accept me, warts and all. As some of you may know, I not only follow "a different drummer," I sometimes hang with the entire brass section of the band. So, my meeting Jane was a miracle. She is smart, talented, and kind. She shares her family with me, lets me spoil her grandkids, knows when we will be alone for Thanksgiving and casually, oh so casually, has us come over to be with her crew. She loves dogs as much as I do, and she let me cry over Bridget, my old Golden Retriever, many times before I accepted it was time to end her suffering. We talk openly about our families and have similar opinions as to how to handle their many crises.

I may as well say this now. If you are my friend, then you become my family, and I will protect you, regardless of whether you need, or want, my help.

Jane has cancer. She has been fighting it for years. When I got cancer, Jane was the first person, after my family, I told. She was a font of information as to what to expect, which products helped, however minimally, and some ways to relieve the weird side effects of Tamoxifen, the medication I would be taking for at least five, possibly more, years to come.

She was and continues to be amazingly, staunchly matter of fact and brave about her own cancer.

Yesterday, I had my annual oncologist appointment. The bloodwork had come back strong, and after an exhaustive exam, the MD said, "I don't want to see you for two years."

I didn't get it. I sort of joked saying, "Was it something I said?" Then I did get it.

The first person I wanted to tell was Jane. But now, she is family and I love her.

I would never hurt her. How could I? But more, how could I not be honest? How could I not share my good news with my dear friend?

I told her, and she was happy for me.

I'm such a jerk.

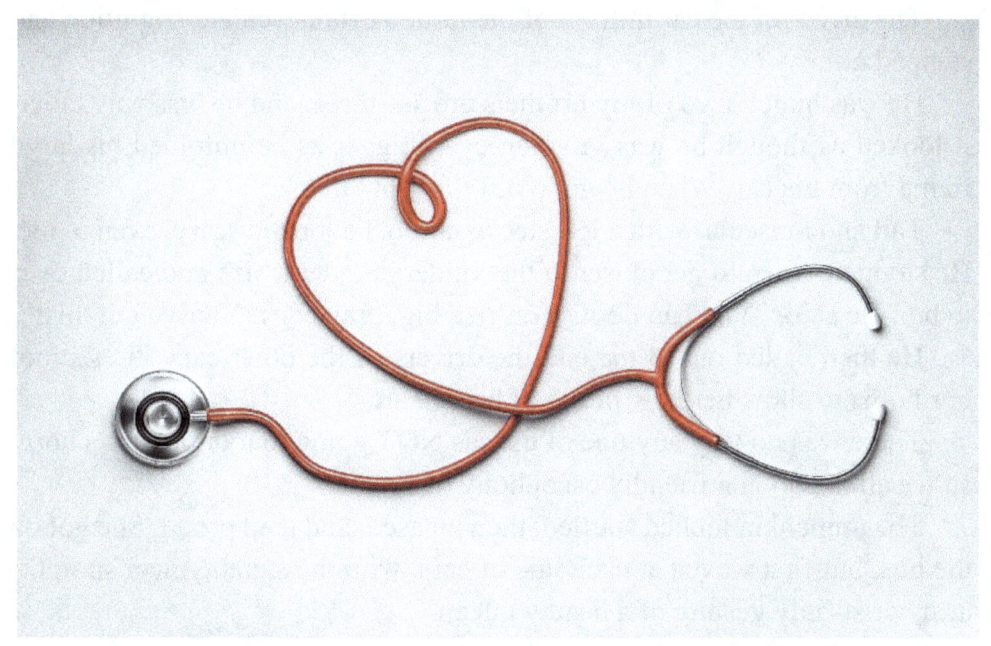

A SCHOOL BUS, A KINDERGARTENER, AND A MAN WITH TATTOOS

On a sunny morning two weeks ago, I was in my car, the second in a line, facing a stopped school bus.

The driver had the bus's lights flashing, and there were two cars behind it. A small child had been waiting with her mother there, holding her hand. When the bus's door opened, the little girl walked toward it, but then turned, frightened, and ran back to her mother.

The mom tried to get her munchkin to go back to the bus.

The bus driver got out and also tried to convince the kindergartener to get on board, so to speak.

The driver of the car in front of me turned off his vehicle's ignition and stepped out.

He was huge! Two of my brothers are six-three, and he was way taller. It looked as though he was growing even bigger as he unfolded his large frame from his car. When he got out, I thought "uh oh."

Tall and muscular with a left sleeve tattoo, he looked scary, even to me. He stooped down to get closer to the kindergartener's size and called over to her. He said, "You can do it! You're a big, brave girl. You've got this!"

He then called out to me and the drivers of the other cars, "Let's toot our horns to show her how proud of her we are."

There was no way any one of us was NOT going to toot our car's horn, so we all did so in a friendly cacophony of sound.

The munchkin looked startled, then pleased, and then proud. She got on the bus, but first waved at each line of cars, with the stereotypical straight-arm, wrist-only gesture of a beauty queen.

I was too caught up in what had just happened to thank that sweet, gentle man for making her day and mine.

He gave each of us drivers a special morning smile.

He gave that tiny princess one too.

GRANDMA'S RECIPE FOR HAPPINESS

There was something about Baking Day.
The kids used to come home from school, on time, on Wednesdays.
Their friends often offered them rides home on Wednesdays.
Paul never worked late on Wednesdays.
The house would be warm and smell amazing.
Everyone would be in a good mood on Wednesdays.
Then, one by one, the kids went off to college.
There would be fewer and fewer of their pals dropping by.
Then they were all gone, having moved on to their adult lives.
But then weddings happened, and spouses and grandkids arrived.
And Wednesdays at our house became popular again.
As a grandma, I learned to bake other families' favorite sweets.
I also learned to never put nuts into desserts, because of some of the children's allergies.
The grandkids began to visit on Wednesdays.
Their friends often offered them rides to their grandma's house on Wednesdays.
Grandpa Paul retired and made them lattes on Wednesdays.
But then sports and extracurricular activities began.
And the grandkids stopped coming over.
It's been months since any of our kids or grandkids visited our house.
This makes sense. Since we are only two, it's easier for us to visit them.
I didn't realize how much things had changed until yesterday when
I made cookies with nuts. I made an apple crumble with nuts, and I realized I don't want to bake anymore.

FUN WITH WORDS

It was my mom who first got me interested in unusual word phrases, although for some of them, I was a tad too literal to "get" the implied sarcasm. One of her favorites used to scare the heck out of me.

For example, I'd run into the house to tell Mom that Ginger or Pat had fallen out of a tree, and Mom would say, "Oh well, Dear, that's one less mouth to feed."

When we moved to Plymouth, I became a docent at the Pilgrim Hall Museum. Thinking to make my tours more interesting, I looked up idioms with historic beginnings.

Unfortunately, most of them were either from later in our country's history or were not part of our history at all.

Take the idiom "dead as a door nail." In colonial times, iron was very expensive. If someone wished to show wealth, he would have nails driven, in an artistic pattern, into the outer door of his home. The nails would go through the door, and then, on the other side, their tips would be bent down. If someone later tried to straighten the bent nails, they would break. Hence the expression, "dead as a door nail."

I learned this next one from a tour guide at an estate in England. In earlier times, the dining table was called "the board." Not everyone who dined had a chair. Some would stand, others might have a place on a bench, and the really important guest would get the solitary chair at the head of the table, or "board." Hence the expression "chair-man of the board."

Another expression that has to do with the word "board" had its origins with men playing cards. If a man held his cards "below the board," it would be assumed he was cheating. If he held them "above the board," he would be assumed to be honest, or "above board."

In Salem, MA, a docent at their historic jailhouse claimed the expression "standing room only" originally referred to the packed jail cells during their infamous witch trials and not to theaters at all.

Actually, I found one saying that is historically correct, although it was a nursery rhyme. I'm sure you remember it.

Pease porridge hot.
Pease porridge cold.
Pease porridge in the pot
nine days old.
Some like it hot.
Some like it cold.
Some like it in the pot nine days old.

The seventeenth-century English sailors enjoyed what was called "Mariners' fare" or "Pease porridge." Somewhat like ratatouille, it was a dish prepared in a caldron-like pot. The first day, a portion of the meal would be consumed. The next day, and those following, the leftovers would be reheated and more ingredients would be added, hence the "Pease porridge in the pot nine days old."

I'll show myself out.

WHEN?

Years ago, I read a short story in which the main character kept murmuring "When?" in a puzzled voice. It is later revealed that she has memory issues, but that wondering character could easily be me.

When did I become unfazed by unexpected weekend company, friends, and family who arrive with salivating kids and laughing dogs?

When did Paul and I develop an unspoken communication system, in which each of us knows exactly what the other is not saying?

When did I acquire enough physics to help my track team kids increase the lengths of their long jumps? (Simply put, greater velocity, plus greater height, equals greater distance)

When did my siblings start asking me for help? They are all better, smarter, kinder people than I will ever be.

When did I stop caring what my "I know everything" friends, who love to correct everyone, say?

When did I become so protective of Paul, that I needed to have a loud discussion with a neighbor who made a caustic remark at his expense. Paul is well able to take care of himself. (I don't, however, think she will be trying that again, any time soon...)

When did I realize that my children aren't perfect? That my grandchildren aren't perfect? That their behavior is not a reflection on me or my parenting?

I sometimes forget, as I watch my grandkids, seemingly growing so rapidly, almost exponentially, that I too am still growing. Just because I can't put my finger on when I learned something, doesn't mean it didn't occur.

I think, as long as we keep trying new and different things, we can all continue to grow, just like our ears.

OUR HOLIDAY GET TOGETHER

Last Tuesday, I was sitting in the conference room smugly surveying all the amazing things I had brought to our holiday gathering.

Nine individually wrapped chicken salad sandwiches, check.

Eighteen individually wrapped home-made, iced sugar cookies, check.

Paper plates and napkins, check.

My homework, a clever monologue written and delivered by a horse, check.

I was so early, I had time to ponder some of the deeper mysteries of life, like in kith and kin, what does kith mean? And why do dogs perspire through their tongues? And who made up the idiotic word petticoat? Seriously, a petticoat is neither petti nor a coat.

I was surprised that I was the only member of our writers' circle to arrive early. Usually a few of us come in before the meeting starts, so we can grab a quick cup of coffee or tea. At eleven o'clock, in the still-empty room, I wondered if I had told everyone we would meet at my house?

As I was leaving the conference room, I noticed that its current schedule was posted on the door. For some reason, our time slot was empty. What the heck was going on?

There was a nice couple in the great room reading their newspapers. They noticed my worried look and asked if something was wrong. I explained that our December meeting was usually a holiday party and that for some reason, no one had shown up.

The man nodded sagely and asked if our December meeting was usually held in November.

November? What? No way was I a week early, was I? At least now I could see why I was the only person in the great room wearing a reindeer headband and red nose. I had to laugh. Everybody else was laughing, so I had to pretend I thought all of this was funny. I walked around the clubhouse giving out chicken salad sandwiches and iced sugar cookies.

I think the people there enjoyed their unexpected treats. They weren't as happy to hear my horse's monologue, but, I guess, some people just aren't into horses.

"GOOD FENCES MAKE GOOD NEIGHBORS" ~ROBERT FROST

Paul and I and our little family lived most of our lives in a small lake town in northern New Jersey. We moved there for the schools and stayed there for the friendships.

When our kids were in their teens, we bought a hot tub. Paul didn't like the fact that our hot tub, not to mention our teenage daughters in their swimsuits, were clearly visible from the street. So, he, our son Jim, and our Papa, dug footings, placed them in concrete, and erected an unstained, natural, stockade fence.

The fence was attached to the house and L-shaped. It was bordered by a small corpse of trees.

Since its parts came in eight-foot segments, its entire expanse was approximately thirty-two feet, with the part shielding the hot tub and our family members from view, eight feet long.

After a weekend blast during which we enjoyed our "private" little Eden, we got a knock on the door.

It was the town building inspector. It seems a part of his job description was to drive around Mountain Lakes checking for violations of town rules. We had erected a fence in violation of the town's "No fences make good neighbors" rule.

The following weekend Paul, Jim, and Papa removed the terrible eye sore, which had taken them a weekend to erect.

Two weeks later, there was another knock on our door. An emissary of the town's safety commission gently but firmly told us that if we had a hot tub, or swimming pool, according to the town's safety codes, we needed to have a fence.

We lived in Mountain Lakes, New Jersey for twenty-five years. For the most part, we enjoyed the foibles of small-town life, fences notwithstanding.

And it turned out, if the top of our hot tub had a locking mechanism, and if we locked the hot tub whenever it was not in use, then the town would allow us to forego building another fence.

BATHROOM GRAFITTI

We were a family of five: Paul, me, and our three children, ages four, three and brand new.

New kids on the block, so to speak, we wanted to introduce ourselves. So, we decided to have a party. We called it a "bring a dish to pass" get together. On the invitations, we stipulated that the invitees were also to bring some graffiti, PG rated, if possible." Graffiti was the hook.

One of my many loves had always been decorating, and I needed help with the tiny, closet-sized bathroom next to our family room. It had a loo, a sink, a mirror, and a towel bar. There wasn't room for anything more.

From that bathroom's ceiling, I hung bold colored markers on long strings. Each guest was to print his or her graffiti on his or her choice of surface. The location and color choice of the clever raunchiness was up to the individual.

Fortunately, our house had two other bathrooms, because it was "standing room only" in the tiny main floor one. As the night went on, and people, especially the guys, warmed up to the idea, they remembered more and more funny bon mots, some of which were not PG rated . . .

One or two of our guests had the misconception that the bathroom could still be used for its everyday purpose. Guys would open the door on their seated wives, and say things like "Close your eyes, Honey. I have to write this down before I forget it." We heard more than one embarrassed shriek come from there as the evening went on.

Here are a few of the quips that were PG rated:
I like grills. That's girls, stupid.
What about us grills?
No laughing at farts!
What's the difference between a hippo and a Zippo?
A hippo is heavy, and a Zippo is a little lighter.
Four out of five stars. I would pee here again.
Don't force it.
I love Charles Dickens.

The party was a big hit. The bathroom was too, until our son Jim began to read and ask questions.

HOW MATURE ADULTS ARGUE

Now married more than fifty years, Paul and I have whittled the fine art of loud discussions down to only the most logical, mature, reasons for using our outdoor voices.

MEALS:

When we moved to Cape Cod in the early years of his retirement, Paul made the statement that I didn't seem to be interested in cooking any more. I rejoined with, "Off of the top of your head, list three meals I make that are your favorites." He shook his head and, in silence, left the room.

LOADING THE DISHWASHER:

If I load the dishwasher, and Paul is around, he will reload it in a more logical manner. When I stopped loading the dishwasher, he thought I was becoming lazy. I told him I was saving energy that was being wasted.

Mine.

GROCERY SHOPPING:

If I am going to the store, Paul will ask to see my list. When I comply, he will then itemize the places and things I will be looking for, explaining that if I follow his numbers, I won't be wasting time or gas by illogically retracing my steps.

MUSICAL TASTE:

Paul doesn't like the same kind of music I do. Oh, we do have some of the same favorites, but my having siblings up to ten years older than me gave me the opportunity to listen to and enjoy the sounds of the '50s.

Since my mom was a pianist, I grew up with classical music.

Since my dad collected big band era records, I love Glen Miller, Artie Shaw, Tommy Dorsey, and Benny Goodman.

I believe you can see where I'm going with this. And I haven't even mentioned that my oldest sister was/is a lyric soprano.

When Paul uses my truck, he is usually very considerate, filling up the gas tank, checking tire pressure, getting it washed, etc. This last time he borrowed my vehicle, he switched out my favorite channels on Sirius Radio to his favorite channels on Sirius Radio (1980's and '90's hits, stock reports, talk radio, and sports programming). It took me a while to put my choices back.

Maturely, calmly, I asked him not to do this again, and he said he wouldn't. He actually seemed surprised that I cared as much as I obviously did.

One might think, since I am a calm, mature person, I would have left it at that. But, in fact, it took me an hour last night to switch all the channels in his Acura MDX to opera, fifties music, classical piano, big band sounds, and Kids Rock.

Maturity is overrated.

"A ROSE BY ANY OTHER NAME . . ."

For most of his corporate career, Paul worked for a German Chemical Company. It became the norm for me to entertain the wives of the "visiting bigwigs" of the firm. They were always intelligent, amazing women. One of their issues, though, was with the vagaries of the English language.

I'm sure you remember George Bernard Shaw's famous quote about the English language. He said, "In America they haven't spoken it for years." Be that as it may, I told the visiting "corporate" lady friends they could call me any time they had a question about our crazy American/English language, and that I would be happy to work with them to explain what I could.

Beautiful Kyoko Yamauchi, from the Island of Honshu, with her new German husband, was my first English Language apprentice. She asked me, "Jonnie, why you call your baby vega'table?"

She believed I was insulting my child, Stephanie, who was three. I wracked my brain to try to figure out what the heck she was talking about. Then I remembered that I had called Stephanie 'pumpkin.' Explaining this took a bit of time, a few laughs, and a bunch of cups of tea, but eventually she accepted that 'pumpkin' was a term of endearment.

Weeks later, I got a phone call from a lady friend from Brussels, whose husband was working in the USA with my husband. She had been driving on the highway and encountered an accident. Listening to the radio, she heard the expression "plastic throating." Apparently, the cars driving past the accident were slowing down to gawk and were causing a delay.

"Jonnie," she asked. "This 'plastic throating' is it an American expression?" I have to admit, for a bit, I was stumped. Then I realized she was translating the word phrase, 'plastic throating' one word at a time. Can you guess what she was asking about?

It was "rubber necking."

Try saying that three times fast. Now try explaining the concept to an amazing woman who speaks three languages to your (almost) one.

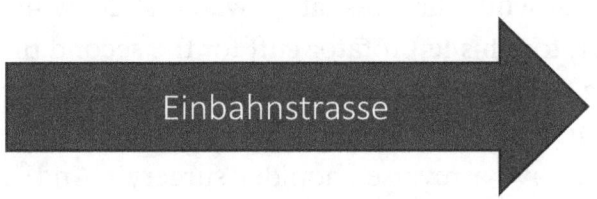

On a business trip to Germany with Paul, I was "allowed' to drive myself around the city of Manheim. I parked the car and took note of the address. I wrote down 'Einbahnstrasse,' which means 'one-way street.' Paul laughed at me.

But my wonderful Japanese, European, lady friends did not.

They empathized. But, more, they loved me almost as much as I loved them.

SOMEONE WHO SHOWS UP

Paul's definition of a friend has always been, "He shows up."

I would take exception to this, asking about shared memories, loyalty, and love ... but he would insist that we were talking about the same thing.

This month, Paul had a reverse shoulder surgery. An accident, which occurred while he was at a water slide with our youngest granddaughter, tore his left rotator cuff for the second time.

When we finally got an appointment with a young, bright, orthopedic, surgeon, he told us, "I can't repair it. (The rotator cuff) You'll have to have a reverse shoulder surgery. (And) I no longer do that particular procedure."

So, back at square one, we began looking for orthopedic surgeons who did do that particular procedure.

Paul had to wait from July until October to get someone to take on his injury. His friends said, "Dude, a water slide? And you're what, seventy?"

But Paul defended himself.

Our granddaughter, Genny, was ten. He couldn't let her go by herself.

Bear with me, as I try to justify my original disagreement with Paul's definition of a friend ...

Our neighbors "showed up." There was stew, soup, pumpkin bread, meatballs and marinara sauce, bagels from New Jersey, and mac and cheese, that all arrived at our door. Bob and Joe stopped by to ask Paul if he wanted to go for a walk. Bill mowed the lawn and picked up our pine needles. Jim mowed and cleared his lawn and a goodly portion of ours, too.

And on and on it went. Our wonderful neighbors "showed up."

Paul was right.

I'd appreciate it if you didn't mention that I said that.

COMFORT FOOD? I THINK NOT.

As I'm sure you know, meals in a large family are not always gourmet fare. The fact that I am from a large family is sometimes lost on Paul, my "only child" husband.

And, although our dinners had to feed a cast of thousands, they were not always beloved. For example, I really, really do not like liver or beef stew.

I am happy to make, and consume, chicken pot pie, shepherd's pie, pizza, homemade lasagna, chicken soup, and nearly any variant of meat and potatoes. (I AM Irish) But I draw the line at most any stew.

Paul loves Polish food but not all Polish foods, i.e., kielbasa and pierogis are okay, but borscht is not. Knowing this, one would think he would get my antipathy for beef stew.

When Paul was working in Corporate America, he often cooked dinner for us on Sundays. He felt doing this relieved stress. He looked for exotic recipes and enjoyed the challenge of new and different cuisines.

He has this habit of turning up his nose to meals I enjoy, calling them "peasant food." Mac and cheese? Ghastly. Hamburgers? Not worth the calories. Grilled cheese sandwiches? Oh, pull yourself together…

Last weekend he decided to make beef stew. The ingredients were fabulous, not just meat and potatoes, there were pearl onions, peas, carrots, and stewed tomatoes. The piece de resistance? Red wine.

I had chicken soup.

He was hurt that I didn't even try his amazing fare.

I said, "Liver with bacon is still liver. Beef stew with red wine is still beef stew. And, as far as I am concerned, a waste of red wine."

We're eating out tonight.

MY AMAZING GARDENING SKILLS

Some people have what we euphemistically call a "Green Thumb." I do not have one. In fact, one of my friends thinks I have what she calls a "Black Thumb." She may be right because my greatest skill with flora is deadheading. I go out early each morning to take care of my daylilies.

It breaks my heart that each flower only blooms for one day. I know, I know, hence the name, "day lily," but the optimist in me keeps trying to help them live, and flower, longer. I give them pep talks, hand water them, and feed them the gourmet plant food of Miracle Grow weekly.

In the beginning of my deadheading apprenticeship, Paul nearly had me convinced my charges were dying of boredom because they had to listen to me telling the same stories over and over again. Aghast, I looked up their phyla. Lucky for me, this was not true. If it were, not only would my flowers be long gone, but so would my children and their children.

Funny, Paul. Real funny.

Now that I think of it though, my sister Puss, Mary Ellen to the uninitiated, is a master gardener. She's won prizes for her tomatoes, her floral arrangements, and her volunteer work helping to keep a local cemetery blooming. When I visit her, she deftly keeps me from getting near her prized blooms. In fact, I have to sit on her garden bench when she weeds and cares for her progeny. And she prefers silence when she works, specifically, my silence. She calls the small area around her home her "Peaceful Garden."

As if that pitiful excuse fools me.

I do have plants all over my house, but most of them are silk. I try to keep my talking to my real ones brief, just in case there is a grain of truth to Paul's little joke... I mostly say things like, "How are you feeling today?" and "Excuse me while I check your roots."

I know it's silly, but sometimes I feel it's a little intrusive to grope around in a plant's soil, so I always apologize when I do, just in case I'm being offensive.

Some of you may have noticed my conscious omission of any

discussion of Paul's American Beauties. He planted them next to my daylilies. As some of you may know, I am not a fan of roses. But I couldn't NOT talk to them after all the bubbling enthusiasm I had just shared with my pretties. So, I began to say fun things to them like, "Nice color, Pink; do you sing too?" and joking a little more, "Hey, Bud! How's it going?" I think they were healthier and more colorful this summer than they have ever been. Paul can thank me later.

To end this on a philosophical note, aren't we homo sapiens fortunate to have the opportunities to bloom more than once?

WHAT PAPA SAID

Whenever Paul and I celebrated a milestone, like an anniversary or a birthday, our papa would say, "The first (add a year here) years are the hardest." And he was always right. Even after we hit fifty years of wedded bliss, he was still right.

And, since he was correct so many times, we listened to his other, wise sayings.

"After age 70, your body is going to fall apart. Oh, you can fake it until then, but it's going to happen."

Sadly, Papa was right.

WHY I DON'T ALLOW GUNS IN OUR HOUSE

Two weeks ago, Paul came down with a horrific cold. He had upper respiratory and pulmonary issues. His coughing, sneezing, and nose blowing sounds reverberated throughout our house.

He wasn't able to sleep because his coughing kept him awake. He wasn't able to play pickleball because he felt so awful. He didn't want to eat because he couldn't taste anything. In short, he was miserable.

My suggestions that he might want to go to our doctor fell on deaf ears. He preferred to suffer.

Then he got better.

This week I came down with Paul's cold. Of course, I've had a much easier time of it. Sadly, my coughing, sneezing, and hoarse, cackling voice disturbed him so he had to move into the guest bedroom so he could get some sleep.

This seemed like a good idea to both of us, because then I could try to sleep sitting up, and I wouldn't have to worry about him losing sleep, because of my loud, annoying cough.

We had planned a dinner party with some friends the following week, as we figured I would probably be better by then.

That morning, when I emerged from our bedroom, still coughing and wheezing, clutching a small wastebasket full of soggy tissues, he asked me, "Are you planning to use linen napkins for the dinner party?"

CHECK THE OIL

Last week I went on a Boston daytrip with two women who really know the city. Since we were in the car for four hours, (going and coming) our conversations ran the gamut from the sublime to the ridiculous. I really enjoyed the ridiculous ones. Sue and Peg's best stories were about their parents' favorite sayings, aka, their parents' "momisms," and "dad-isms."

Some of the funnier sayings were made even more so when we realized that our parents, from three different cultures, three different generations, and three different states, had nearly the exact same wisdom to impart.

Here are the momisms we shared:

1. "I don't care who started it."
2. "Why? Because I said so, that's why."
3. "If everybody else jumped off a cliff, (or bridge) would you do it too?"
4. "Sue, Peg, Ginger, whatever your name is . . ."
5. "I'm going to give you until the count of three."

Here are the dad-isms we shared:

1. "Turn off those lights. Do you think I'm made of money?"
2. "Close the door, you're letting all the heat out. Do you live in a barn?"
3. "Whatever you do, don't tell your mother."
4. "Don't forget to check your oil."
5. "You're not going out dressed like that."

What made us laugh even more, was the fact that each of us has begun to say at least one of these quotes before stopping in mid-spiel, horrified, to realize we have become our parents . . .

My mom had another maxim that I hated as a teen, but which has escaped my lips more than once when I lectured my daughters and, worse, my granddaughters. She would say, "(Insert name here), your clothing should be tight enough to show you're a woman, but loose enough to show you're a lady . . ."

When Paul got his driver's license, his mother told him to "Always wear clean underwear, in case you're in an accident."

Paul and I didn't need to remember our parents' sayings, as we were perfectly capable of making up our own . . .

"At a party, always learn where the doors are, so if things go south, you can get out quickly."

"Call us anytime, and we will pick you up, no questions asked."

And, "Don't forget to check the oil."

ANNOYING? MOI?

After three years of dating and fifty-two years of marriage, Paul has discovered that I have some irritating habits. The poor man has been confined to quarters, with me, for four weeks since his reverse shoulder operation.

In the normal scheme of things, he would be working out every morning, playing pickleball four days a week, and having a few pick-up golf games. Since his surgery, on October the 24th he has watched every Hallmark Christmas story ever made, memorized all the stock information and quotes on Squawk Box, and learned that Alexa can tell us what the weather is anywhere in the world, any hour of the day ...

When he first retired from corporate America, Paul seemed to be at a loss. At that time, he alphabetized my spices, set up my linen closet so the sheets were in descending order of size, and helped me run errands by numbering the places I was going to patronize. He did that so I would drive in a circular route, and, not go back and forth, in a zig zag pattern wasting time and gas.

One day, still newly retired, he asked me to mail a few letters, which I did. When I returned home, he asked if I had mailed them.

"Yes," I replied.

"What time did you mail them?" he asked.

"Around noon," I said.

"I wanted them to go out in the morning mail!" he barked. "Kay would have made sure they went out then."

Kay, who had also retired, had been his assistant, and my right arm, when Paul was working.

We would double team him to get him to dentist appointments, to remind him which of our kids had a game and where it would be, and to remind him of birthdays and anniversaries.

So, using her name to reprimand me did not work. I calmly reminded Paul that Kay had been paid a salary to work on his behalf ...

As for my irritating habits, I am always either humming or whistling, sotto voce.

My mom used to do this, too. One day she was laughing as I walked into the kitchen. So, I asked her what was so funny.

She laughed. "Apparently I have been whistling the same tune all morning. Moe came in, trilled a different melody, and I changed my song to his. I just realized what he did."

We smiled at each other, in perfect understanding.

WHAT I DID ON MY SPRING VACATION

When I was teaching, I never asked any of my students to write an essay on "What I did On My Summer Vacation." Even if parents took their kids out of school when we were in session, and asked me for assignments for their offspring, I would always say that going to a different place, even if it was to Grandma's, was an educational experience.

Be that as it may, after Paul and I visited our son Jim's family in Georgia, we went on a brief sojourn to Hilton Head; after which, I felt a new connection with the Lotus-eaters in the Odyssey. (In Greek Mythology, those who ate of the lotus plant never wanted to return home and lived in a state of perpetual indolence.) My experience in Hilton Head was somewhat similar. Since I messed up both of my knees in my youth, because I was such an amazing athlete, I neither play golf nor tennis, nor pickleball . . .

Let me share my arduous holiday regimen with you:

MORNING:
Get up. Have a cup of tea. Drive to a coffee shop and buy breakfast. Walk a mile on a stunning, beautiful beach. Return to our vacation rental. Rest from difficult beach trek.

NOON:
Go to pool. Bring the book I've been planning to read for a year. Begin to read book; nap with same on my chest. Wake up. Return to rented condo. Change.

NIGHT:
Go out for dinner. Drink wine. Return to condo. Watch a movie or two on Netflix. Drink more wine. Go to bed.

NEXT DAY:
Repeat yesterday's schedule. Add shopping for clothing in colors other than Navy or black. Go out. Wear new clothes. Find another amazing fish restaurant. Drink wine, or, if in a crazy mood, a Margarita. Make small talk

with strangers. Pretend to listen to them. Drink more wine. Wonder why my capris aren't fastening as easily as they did at the beginning of the vacation.

NEXT DAY:
Ditto.

NEXT DAY:
Pack for return home. Think Dorothy was right. Return rental car. Take plane back to MA. Arrive at Logan. Listen to and feel comforted by the people there whose New England attitude is a lot like mine. Get the car from long-term parking. Clear slushy snow from its windshield. Drive back home to Plymouth. Arrive. Notice that the rabbits have been eating our crocus. See that the birds have nested atop our deck's outdoor speakers again, instead of in the two birdhouses Paul made for them. Smile.

Think that the best part of going away for a vacation is coming home again.

THE THINGS WE DO FOR LOVE

Last Wednesday, Paul and I were running around getting everything ready for the five-hour trip to NJ where our daughter Gretchen lives. Her father-in-law had died, and she asked us, if we could come to his memorial service. Of course we said, "Yes."

I got a reservation at a pet-friendly motel because it was too late to get a sitter for Sophie, our Golden. We decided to take my trusty Ridgeline because we were going to return with two dogs, instead of one.

We had planned to watch Gretchen's seven-year-old Yellow Lab, Max, while she and her family went to Europe for ten days. I had promised to do this months ago, and we had already scheduled a time, date, and place for her delivery of, and our receipt of, Max.

Since we were already going to be at her house, we decided to take Max back with us, thus saving Gretchen and Paul their separate trips to Mystic CT, where we usually make our pet swaps.

First, the trip to NJ took us seven hours. We had supper with Gretchen's family, and then returned to our motel, where we both fell face down on the bed.

Then, Miss Sophie, who was not used to an urban environment, especially trucks and their air brakes, stayed up all night, saving us from the rigs, and their drivers, by barking loudly in her "Big Dog Voice."

The next day, the funeral mass was lovely. Everyone gathered outside the church afterward to share condolences and family stories. It was 1 PM by the time the groups of relatives began to break up to head to the scheduled Italian Restaurant for lunch.

Paul looked at me and whispered, "We should probably leave now as the trip might take us seven hours again." I agreed, so we paid our respects, returned to Gretchen's house, changed into casual clothing, picked up the two dogs, and were off.

The five-hour trip didn't take seven hours this time; it took eight. Every vacationer in the Northeast was on the road. We had to stop twice for the dogs (and me). When we arrived in Plymouth, we took the dogs for a walk, fed them, grabbed a white wine for me, a Crown Royal for Paul, and just about fell on our faces again.

What is this thing that we do for our loved ones? Is there a name for it? If it's love, then love is going to kill us.

MY WINTER ADVENTURE

I completely fell apart.

In early January, I had what was called a "cloudy mammogram." Told that I had to schedule a repeat mammogram and a sonogram, I asked the nurse, "When? Tomorrow, next week?" She told me the first date I could get in would be the end of February…

In the interim, because I'd been there, done that, (years ago) I began the mental and physical preparations for the possibility of another lumpectomy.

In the four and a half weeks until the next tests, idiotically, I finished my third book, (which I had been sitting on for months) took three loads of clothing and bedding to Savers and organized my linen closet.

I did the linen closet because I have had this insane idea for years that people might say of me, (when I die) "She was a nice person, but did you see her linen closet?"

I also, bravely, did not tell any of our three adult children about this, thinking nobly, "They have enough on their plates."

All of February, I prepared for the worst-case scenario, going through bureaus, emptying closets and cupboards. In short, getting ready to be out of commission for a while.

The 27th of February, I had my second mammogram and first ultrasound. Both were negative. There was nothing terrible for me to face. When I got home, I told Paul everything was all right, that I was Okay. But for some reason I wasn't.

Why? I have no idea.

Prepared to be brave, and face the worst, I wasn't ready to be found healthy. Man, a psychologist would have a field day with this.

Me not so much.

YOU'RE NOT THE BOSS OF ME

At our monthly family Zoom meeting, I was laughingly telling my siblings that my writing group calls me *The Boss of the World*. I then noticed that no one else was laughing.

"What? I asked. (a tad defensively)

They said I was always giving myself titles like that.

"No way!" said I." Name one!"

And so, the litany began:

President of the Igneous Rock Club (Igneous rocks were formed by molten lava, so there weren't many to be found in rural Connecticut where we lived. Nevertheless, I felt it was important that we learn about them.)

President of the Bird Club (Bird were cool, so I liked to look for different kinds and to practice saying their names. (Think, Scarlet Tanager, Baltimore Orioles, and the Backwards Tuxedo Bird, the Bobolink.)

Queen of "Wadsie's" Pond (a polluted pond, deep in our woods, that our mom had on the forbidden list, but oh, the lure of the forbidden.)

President of the Pat Boone Fan Club (Our parents wouldn't let us, my friend Barbara and me, join the Elvis Presley Fan Club, so we started a Pat Boone one. I'm not sure if I was president or if Barb was…)

"Okay, okay," I said. "Then why, if I was so bossy and tough, did I find the words 'You're Not the Boss of Me' to resonate with me so much I made them the title of my book?" (shameless plug here for my second opus.)

They answered in a chorus, "Because WE said it to you all the time!"

It's sad when people's memories of things are so skewed. I'm going to have to form a therapy club to help them. And, since it's my idea, I get to be president.

FINDING MY VOICE AGAIN

Years ago, when I was young and, well, young, I loved Mama Cass's song. "Make Your Own Kind of Music." I always felt she was singing to me.

She sang, "Make your own kind of music. Sing your own special song. Make your own kind of music, even if no one else sings along."

For some reason, this was easier to do when I was younger and, well, younger. Now, I find I'm less willing to embarrass Paul, although I still do it, just not on purpose. I'm less willing to call out behavior I know is caustic, somehow hoping to keep the peace.

However, (you knew this was coming right?) I am finding I don't have the patience to wait for my friends to show up. You're busy? Okay. So will I be next time you ask me for a favor.

I have children and grandchildren who need me to show them, by my example, how to stand up for themselves. And how to sing their own songs…

So, I'm going to begin, again, to "make my own kind of music, sing my own special song. Make my own kind of music," and my family and friends damn well better sing along.

NO PLACE LIKE HOME

My friend is moving. There are many reasons for this change of location, suffice it to say being closer to her children and grandchildren played a major part in her decision to sell.

Her real estate agent had numerous "suggestions" as to how to make her home more appealing to prospective buyers:
1. No family memorabilia, especially photographs
2. No corny magnets on the fridge
3. No silk flowers, current buyers don't like them
4. No pet accessories, beds, toys, leashes, or bowls for food
5. No pets
6. No grandchild-made anything. It was all to be put away for "another day."
7. No candles

From what I gathered, nothing in any way reminiscent of their life well-lived here for twenty-plus years may be seen. I know I'm not "there yet," but my house is my home until it isn't. If John, or Joan, Q Public wants a sterile place to call home, he/she should go buy a doctor's office.

My husband Paul bought our third house. I hadn't seen it. When I was able to check it out, I found the décor awful, the architecture basic, and parts of the house in need of work.

The proud mother of three children under five, I had trusted Paul to make a good decision. And he did. The house exuded warmth, and happiness, and familial love. I could clearly see the homeowners were loath to leave. The awful gold-fringed draperies did not, in any way, diminish the overall vibes that were telling us this would be a good place to raise our kids.

I refuse to believe individuals searching for their next home will be unable to see past a lopsidedly printed "HuRAY for Grimma" Mother's Day card or a six-year old's drawing of flowers for Valentine's Day that in no way resembled any flora found on this planet.

Real estate agents looking for the biggest bang for their buck are overlooking the charm of an old dog napping on a sunny deck, or a puppy's enthusiastic welcome. I would guess, since I don't have to move, I can be as independent as I want. My friend doesn't have that option.

And maybe, just maybe, having to put cherished memories and memorabilia away, in a box or out of sight, will make the move easier when it happens. I don't know. /Let's ask a REALTOR®.

DON'T LET THE DOOR HIT YA ON THE WAY OUT

It's funny how a few extra hours in each other's company can become a bone of contention.

When Paul had his pickleball accident and was unable to play for three weeks, I thought I would kill him, or at the very least, hurt him more than his rib-breaking-lung-piercing fall did.

We'd gotten into the routine of at least three hours a day spent apart. (Sophie, the dog, doesn't count in this particular space/time continuum.)

When Paul plays, pickle or golf, I have options. If golf, I get five hours to take a room down to its bones, and either clean it, paint it, or cull it of its ephemera. If pickleball, I get three hours to give myself a facial, launder winter clothing and put it away, or move *objet d'art* to new places in the house.

I'm betting Paul has come to appreciate his alone time, too.

Two adults of a certain age, no matter how loving, no matter how caring, need time away from each other. After fifty (or so) years together, they know each other's likes, dislikes, stories, and opinions. I'm sure you can see how a few hours apart will give them something new to say, something new that has happened, and a new joy or annoyance to share.

Paul doesn't need to hear (again) that he should empty the pockets of his jeans before he puts them in the laundry. I do not need to hear him say (again), "You've said that a million times already."

His latest injury, a bad back, has had me frantically searching for things to do, places to go, people to see…

And I feel like a rat.

I love this man. But as my art teachers used to say, "Sometimes less is more."

And I'm pretty sure, he, more or less, feels the same.

PARENTS:

HOW TO RAISE THEM

YOUR EYES ARE BIGGER THAN YOUR STOMACH

As you might expect, my parents had some unique rules regarding food, its various uses, and my siblings and my involvement with same.

We had to clean our plates.

We had to eat all of our vegetables before we could touch whatever meat was on the menu.

We were often told that our eyes were bigger than our stomachs, something I didn't understand.

If you consider the sheer number of groceries our mother purchased and prepared for the ten of us kids, then her rule that we clean our plates makes sense.

We had to eat all of our vegetables before we could even consider touching the meat portion of the meal. I still do this, and it makes Paul crazy.

I knew my eyes weren't "bigger than my stomach." I knew because, when I was ten, I checked them out in the bathroom mirror. I thought Mom was just being silly. Ginger tried to explain this expression to me, but I still knew Mom was wrong.

As young entrepreneurs, we learned to barter our way through the dreaded vegetable portion of our meals. Sandie loved asparagus. I did not. I liked broccoli; she did not. So we worked out an amicable solution. Sandie always ate my asparagus. Even at Ginger's wedding, when we were in our twenties, she silently slipped her bread plate under the table to me, so I could unload my asparagus. Man, I loved Sandie.

Another thing we did as kids was to check in with each other before dinner.

What was it going to be?

Who hated which part? Brussel Sprouts were always a loser.

Who would be willing to swap, and for what?

As an adult, I still find myself obeying my parents' rules. I still try to finish whatever is on my plate, even if I don't like the food, even if I'm not hungry, even if Paul is eying the fries I ordered and don't want...

My parents have a lot to answer for.

MOM STORIES, WE ALL TELL THEM

Sandie, Mike, Pat, and I were checking out our baby brother Chris's belly button.

It was an "outie," whereas all of ours were "innies." Our mom came into the room to find us lifting up our undershirts to compare ours to his. She asked me, as I was the oldest, at seven and a half, of our little quartet what were we doing.

"We're comparing belly buttons, Mom," I said. "Is Chris going to be okay? I mean, having an 'outie,' belly button, is that bad?"

She assured us he was going to be fine.

"Okay," said I. "What does a belly button do? I mean, how did we get belly buttons?"

Mom said, "When He finished making you, God poked each of you in the tummy." Mom demonstrated. "Then," she said, "He said, 'You're done. You're done. You're done.'" Made sense to us.

Another time, while we were playing with our latest batch of kittens, Sandie asked Mom, "How can you tell which ones are boys?"

Mom didn't hesitate a second. She said, "The boys have whiskers."

Mom's repertoire of stories and clever explanations might not have been original to her, but she used them with amazing age-appropriate timeliness.

I'm still shaking my head over our easy acceptance of her answers. We believed most of them.

All striped cats got an "M" on their foreheads from the Blessed Mother? Yep. I looked that one up in our encyclopedia and found out even tigers have an "M" on their foreheads. Mom was right! The Blessed Mother was awesome!

God put (Irish) blue eyes in with a "dusty finger" because he didn't wash his hands after creating the world for six days? Uh huh. (The dusty finger made eyebrows and eye lashes especially dark and lush) God was probably tired . . .

Mom's timing was also legendary. She would lick the knife she had been using to frost a birthday cake and say, "Now children, I only do this to show you what you should never do. Licking knives is dangerous."

I sometimes feel in this era of telling children "the whole truth," we forget that imagination and humor can be a good stopgap. At the age of seven, I should have figured out the "belly button truth." After all, I had four younger siblings, but Mom knew when I got it, I would think her silly answer was funny.

I'll admit I've told my kids some "Mom stories" when the answers to their questions could have been over their pointed little heads. When Jim asked me if there was a rock in his knee, I said, "You are such a smartie to figure that out."

I was nursing baby Stephanie when Gretchen asked, "If there's milk in one of those," pointing to my chest, "is there juice in the other one?" I said, "Yes, yes there is."

Reality comes so soon, I wanted for them what my mom wanted for us, a little more time in Childhood Land.

BTW: Chris's belly button is still an "outie." He says it isn't, but none of the rest of us wants to check.

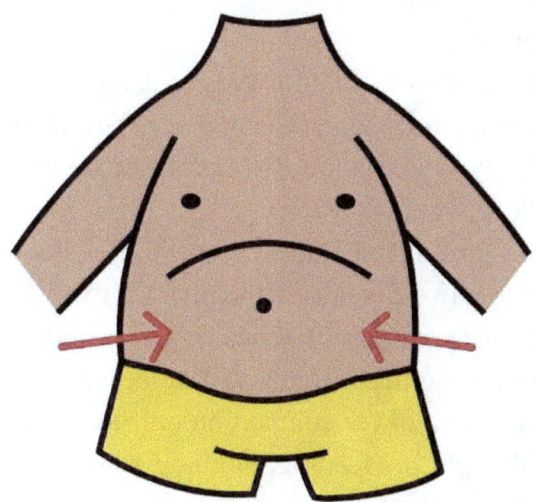

How Not to Manage Money

My dad, who was always the first to remind us that he was a genius; was also always the first to admit that his money management skills were dismal.

When I used to ask my siblings how many acres we owned when we lived in Norwalk, CT, their answers always differed. Recently, we figured out why. When our parents bought Stoneybrook, the house came with six acres. But, whenever a decent amount of extra cash was needed, our dad would sell off an acre.

The monies from his first sale, to the Ryan family, paid a good deal of Joe's tuition at Fordham University.

The Tolland family's purchase? Moe's time, however brief, at Boston College.

The Virgel's? Ginger's tuition at Georgetown Visitation . . .

For a long time, Dad held fast to the land (two acres) that held our regulation-size baseball field. It was his "baby." Once he was sure we were moving, he sold that too. When we sold our house, it was situated on an acre of land, hence the sixth acre.

Question answered.

Once in Ohio, Dad still had four kids to send on to higher learning. I was already a sophomore at what is now Pace, but Sandie, Mike, Pat, and Chris were bright-eyed and seriously decent students who deserved the opportunities college would provide.

His accountant introduced Dad to something called The Tuition Plan. Dad hated having to pay dividends to the plan for twelve more years, but he did it. Once Chris, the youngest, graduated from school, Dad was liberated. Now he could have some fun with his vast holdings . . .

We, his ten children, never counted on our father leaving us anything. Every one of us thought his feeding, clothing, and educating us was more than enough of an inheritance.

But Dad did leave us something.

My share was enough for me to pay for a semester at Duke for my son Jim.

THE CHURCH AND MOM AND ME

My mom was the consummate Roman Catholic. Her faith was an integral part of who she was.

Church obligations and Latin rhetoric were automatically observed and noted. An example that comes to mind is the fact that she got us, all of her ten children, to attend daily Mass in Lent and Advent, and to say the rosary every night in May, the Month of the Blessed Mother, and October, the Month of the Holy Rosary.

On the other hand, Mom always encouraged us to study, and to question, things we didn't think made sense. She also always accepted the later-in-life faith choices of her adult children, which were, and still are, all over the map. This is a sort of preface to a talk Mom and I had early one morning, when we were making the little kids' school lunches.

I had just finished reading *The Robe* by Lloyd C. Douglas. Historical religious fiction, it told the story of a Roman tribune whose life was profoundly changed when he, an officer, led the garrison of soldiers who crucified Christ. Of course, there was much more to the story, but Mom and I got hung up on the rubrics of the Catholic Church at that time.

Any book, treatise, or article about "religion," was required to have a nihil obstat, imprimatur, if it were to be accepted. This was the Catholic Church's way of censoring religious reading material, even fiction. Nihil obstat means there is "no obstacle" to someone reading a piece.

Imprimatur means "let it be printed."

The Robe did not get this papal blessing.

I asked Mom, "What was the problem in the book?"

She said, she thought it was the way the author described the miracle of the loaves and fishes. Lloyd Douglas wrote that the words of Christ caused a change of heart in his audience; that His message of love caused the crowd of people to share food they had been selfishly hoarding...

Mom continued, "We believe that Christ performed the miracle, that it was His power over nature and the laws of physics that caused the multiplication of the loaves and fishes."

"So what?" I said, "Either way, a miracle occurred. What difference does it make if Jesus's words or his deed effected the miracle? Either way one occurred." I took a breath. "Besides, Mom, this was fiction. Don't you think the church is going someplace it doesn't belong?"

Mom nodded her head. "Good point," she said.

That was the day I became a "cafeteria Catholic."

THE SIXTH SENSE

I don't claim in any way to have a sixth sense. What I can lay claim to though, is the fact that enough times in my life something or someone made me change what I was doing.

And the results left me shaken but unharmed.

The first time I can recall was when I was vacuuming my daughter's bedroom. We had an in-house vacuum system that was very loud. Something made me turn the vacuum off and go check on my three children.

I went out into the hall to find my four-and-a-half-year-old son Jim trying to stuff his four-month-old baby sister Stephanie down the laundry chute. I pulled the baby back, and looked down three flights to the basement. His other sister, Gretchen, who was three-and-a-half-years old, was waiting there, arms extended, ready to catch the baby. They had been doing this with their dolls, her Barbie, and his GI Joe, and they thought their little sister might enjoy it too.

The second time was when my brand-new car stalled at a green light. I couldn't get the damn thing to start, try though I might. Out of nowhere, an eighteen-wheeler, whose brakes had failed, ran the red light, and careened to a screeching halt two blocks past the intersection. The rig barreled across the road right where I would have been had my car not stalled.

The third time involved a simple change in my routine. I was driving, with our three kids in tow, to our local grocery store. It, the store, was only a mile away from our house, but I decided to take a different route to show the children a local farm's new-born foals. We stopped and looked and laughed at the awkward horse babies jumping and playing.

Later that day, I learned there had been a freak accident on our "road not taken." A huge old tree, with rotten roots, had fallen across the street and its branches had impaled two unfortunate vehicles.

As you can surmise, none of these incidents involved me having ESP. They did, however, involve something or someone protecting me and my family.

Why did I stop vacuuming?

Why did my new car stall?

Why did I feel the kids would want to see the foals that day, that time?

I only know that I will always be grateful for the help given us, whatever the source. Although I'm pretty sure I know who it was.

Mom.

MR. OLIVER AND OUR MOM

When I was very young, my family had a "handyman" who lived with us.

His name was Oliver. My mom wanted us to call him "Mr. Oliver," but he insisted "just Oliver" was fine with him. Oliver had a room off the back porch which had a bathroom and a very small all-purpose space.

According to my mom, Oliver was "shell shocked." I believe now we would say he had some form of PTSD. What that meant, to us, was, he would sometimes go away and return somewhat the worse for the wear. He was going on what our parents called "benders." We kids thought "benders" were some sort of rides.

Our mom always accepted Oliver and his disappearances, so we did too.

I was very young when Oliver didn't come back, but that is another story.

One particular Thanksgiving, my half-English grandfather, Pop, was visiting. Pop had had quite a few drinks. He took exception to Mr. Oliver sitting down to dinner with the family. Pop announced that he didn't sit at table "with the help."

Our mom said, "I'm sorry you feel that way," and continued to serve everyone, including Oliver.

Pop stood up and proclaimed, "Britain will rule the waves again!" and with a flourish, exited the room.

It was quite dramatic. Unfortunately, he lived in New York and we lived in Connecticut, so he needed a ride home. So much for "exiting stage left."

This is a story that was told to me, as I was quite young when this all happened.

When my older siblings talk about it now, they're still amazed that our mom stood firm, as Pop was a formidable person.

I'm not.

Siblings: How Many Is Too Many?

"THERE IS ONLY ONE THING MORE PRECIOUS THAN TIME, AND THAT'S WHO WE SPEND IT WITH."

When we study another language, we sometimes become so busy translating words, we miss their larger meaning. For example, the word phrase *mi casa su casa*'s word-by-word translation into English is, "My house (is) your house." But a Spanish pal once told me the expression's true meaning is, "You are home."

Bear with me, I do have a reason for this vocabulary/life lesson.

My brother Joe's memorial will be held the Saturday after Thanksgiving, in Chelsea, NY.

We, my family, and his widow, have been trying to set a date for this for a while, but Nora was in an accident and has been in rehab for most of a year. Thus Joe's service will be held on the one-year anniversary of his death.

Paul and I had plans to celebrate our wedding anniversary that weekend, in an air BNB in Vermont. Gretchen had plans to celebrate her family's Thanksgiving in Ireland with her daughter, Casey, who is having her semester abroad there. Jim had just taken time off from work to attend my other brother's memorial in Northern California. Stephanie, who usually hosts her in-laws for Thanksgiving is trying to figure out how to do that and still go to Joe's service.

After recently attending a life celebration, my friend Frank and I discussed ways we want to honor our loved ones. He told me about the Japanese word for time, which is *taimu*.

Taimu means much more than the mere passage of years, he explained. Taimu refers to giving the gift of time, which is visiting those we love, listening to their stories, reminiscing, and doing nothing, but doing nothing, together. He and his wife had just returned from a trip to California where they did exactly that with an elderly relative and an old friend.

Going to his memorial will honor Joe. But more, it will give his widow, Nora, and our family, time, and the opportunity to tell "Joe stories," to reminisce, to share a meal, and to do nothing, together.

Taimu, what a wonderful word. I'm going to teach it to my children.

FOR THOSE WE LOVED AND LOST…

"Good God, no! Raise a glass for me, Scotch if you've got it." This was our Papa Joe's response when I asked him, "Dad, is there any charity you would like the family to donate to in your name?"

Paul's dad, our papa, lived with us for seven years. He was always easy to be with, easy to talk to, easy to love. When he turned ninety, he wanted us to be sure we understood his final wishes.

Hence my question and his answer.

Papa died when he was ninety-six years old. At his memorial dinner every single one of us raised a glass of (ugh) Scotch.

"To Papa," Paul said.

"To Papa" we echoed.

My oldest brother Joe died early this month. He kept the family together after our parents died.

In the then pre-Facebook era, he sent each of us, his nine siblings, a questionnaire. We were to fill in the blanks with our names, addresses, birthdates, and anniversaries, everyone's cell phone numbers and all of our landline numbers. Joe then worked his magic and sent the results, by snail mail, to each of us.

He called it Lanes, USA. We used Lanes, USA for years. We still do. Joe kept it current, editing the information every other year. Our youngest brother, Chris, took it one step further and set up a "family only" Facebook site for us. We use that all of the time too.

Two years ago, our niece, Meara, set up a monthly Sunday afternoon Zoom meeting for the rest of us. If you follow the dots, you will see that staying together and keeping together is important to my brothers and sisters and to me.

Our Zoom meeting last month was to say "Goodbye" to Joe, who was in hospice. Although his sense of humor was still strong, his body wasn't. He asked us to have a gin and tonic for him. So, we did.

MY TWO OLDER BROTHERS

My oldest brother, Joe, died last December. My second oldest brother, Moe (Paul Allen), died last week. One would think as we age, that the end phases of life will become more familiar, and somehow easier to understand. I suppose that can be true. But there are holes in the fabric of my family. Our beautiful life quilt is missing two more important pieces.

We were 'the ten.' I always thought of us as invincible. Now we are missing two important players in our familial game of life.

I haven't grieved yet. I'm still caught in an odd limbo.

I used to check in on Moe around eight in the morning. No matter how many times he gently reminded me of the three-hour time difference between Massachusetts and California, he would still take my calls ...

Joe lived in NYC. There was no time difference between the two of us. But him, I would call late at night. I have no idea why.

With Covid's restrictions, we all began to have a once-a-month Zoom call. I have to admit this: it was easier to keep in touch when I couldn't see how my siblings were aging, how we all were aging.

Last Sunday, each of us made a recorded message for Moe, to remind him how much we treasure his wit and intellect and really bad "dad" jokes.

"Why do they cut off the heads of sardines? So, they don't bite each other in the can . . ."

When I look back to Sunday and our corny, loving testimonials, I can accept that the loving messages we sent were as much for us as they were for him.

Enclosed is one of my favorite A. A. Milne quotes. Somehow it always comforts me. I like to think we're all like piglet and Pooh.

"We'll be friends forever, won't we Pooh?" asked Piglet.

"Even longer," Pooh answered.

Joe and Moe, we will be siblings forever. And if Pooh is right, even longer. Rest in Peace Big Brothers.

FAMILY IS EVERYTHING

For the first time in a long time, I'm not sure how to handle a family issue. As you may have surmised, I'm usually pretty sure I know what I'm doing. (Think Davy Crockett, "Be sure you are right, then go ahead.")

My brother Moe died recently. He had lived in Northern California for the last thirty years. The rest of us, his seven remaining siblings, live in six different states, have varying levels of financial stability, and differing health issues. I don't need to enumerate the differing health issues to know that not one of us will be able to attend Moe's memorial.

My son Jim has volunteered to go to represent the family. For the two years, Jim worked in San Francisco, for Anderson Consulting, he spent most of his weekends with Moe and his family. Jim wrote Paul and me saying how much he loved his girl cousins, two gun-toting feminists, whom he said intimidated the hell out of him. Moe gave Jim an uncle with the same weird sense of humor as his mother, me, and the family he needed at the time.

Since Jim would be representing the family. I gratefully said Paul and I would finance his trip.

A dear friend and neighbor suggested that maybe Moe's family would benefit more from the money we would be spending to send Jim to CA, than from his being there. He continued saying, as if he were me, "This is for you, (meaning Moe's widow and his daughters) to use as you see fit, to do something you feel would honor Moe's life."

This made sense to my math brain.

But I couldn't get my heart around it. To me, Jim's going would be an act of affection and gratitude. He loves Moe's family and has been grateful for years for the way they welcomed him, their odd cousin from New England, into their lives.

Years ago, I read *Heidi* by Johanna Spyri. In it, young Heidi went to pick berries for her grandfather. She sold the berries, thinking he would be more pleased with the money than with the fruit. Her grandfather threw the coins to the ground, asking her, "What made you think I would prefer sour metal to the sweet taste of sun-ripened berries?" I read *Heidi* when I was twelve. That lesson, obviously, made quite an impression on me.

So, here I am. I have to decide by tomorrow.

I know what I want to do. Paul says it's up to me, but I sense his opinion is at odds with mine. Tonight, I'm calling my six siblings to get their input, with no promises to listen to any of them.

What would you do?

*All six of my siblings, Chris, Pat, Mike, Gret, Ginger, and Puss said, "Send Jim."

Actually, this is not true. Chris and Gret said, "Send Jimmy."

FOR MY BROTHERS, I LOVE YOU

Brothers are a pain. I know because I grew up with four of them.
I used to think they stayed up nights thinking of new and different
ways to ruin my life.
Adults now, we still annoy the heck out of each other,
especially politically, especially Mike.
Three days ago, he texted us, his six remaining siblings.
I was expecting another banal quip or political meme.
And I was ready...
Not this time.
Mike wrote to tell us that his son Chris was dying.
Now, all I want to do is go and be there for him,
the pain-in-the-ass-little brother that I love unconditionally.
Here's the thing.
I've been writing columns about my family for years.
I even published two books full of their stories.
Now, because of those of you who purchased them,
I have some money I can send Mike.
Of course, Paul insisted on helping. I knew he would.
And, also of course, I will be going out to Ohio. I will be there in person.
I will be able to hug Mike, and I'm pretty sure, after a while, to annoy
    him. That's what sisters do.
But for now, I am grateful for you, my dear friends,
who have given me the means to help him.
RIP Christopher Michael Lane

P.S. Mike wouldn't take a thing.

TURNS OUT WE DID WALK UPHILL BOTH WAYS

My family has once-a-month Zoom gatherings and, as sometimes happens with siblings who are mean and cruel and brats, talk often circles around to the topic of weather and the question as to whose is worse. My sisters Puss and Ginger, who live in Georgia and North Carolina respectively, are usually the ones to bring it up. Personally, I think they like to rub my frost-bitten New England nose in our snowy weather.

This past Sunday, I thought I'd cleverly distract the weather mavens by asking everyone what did they remember us doing when we were growing up in Connecticut and seriously bad weather threatened? They fell for it. And I have to admit I had no idea how much work went in to protecting our family, our house, and our property from "demon-weather."

First the animals had to be brought inside. This was difficult because our barn cats were nearly feral. They did not want to be saved. The dogs, however, would quickly run inside, then upstairs and under the beds of their favorite kids.

The apple and pear trees had to be harvested before any projected gale winds did the job for us. Of course, doing this resulted in fruit battles with multiple bruises and black eyes sustained, that had to be tended to by Mom.

The taps in the kitchen and five bathrooms had to be opened to a slow drizzle to keep the pipes from freezing.

There then had to be a number of trips to the grocery store because everyone knew if the food ran out, we would become cannibals and eat the littlest kids.

The "good" cars had to be put in the garage to protect them from broken branches and flying debris.

On one occasion, we drove Puss's Nash Metropolitan into the living room because strong winds had taken out our electricity, and Daddy needed to hear the news. The floors in the living room were marbleized concrete, so no hardwoods were ruined. The oriental rug on the other hand…

Joe and Moe had to bring in loads of firewood in case the electricity went off. They stacked it by the walk-in fireplace. Even now I think the best, most aromatic fires are made by burning apple wood. Our fireplace was huge, and we sometimes slept in front of it, eight to ten idiots giggling and being silly. We didn't realize just how serious the situation was. I think this was because our mom made it all seem like a grand adventure.

With all the memories being resurrected, discussed, and dissected, ("It did SO happen that way!"), my two mean sisters forgot to remind the rest of us of their sunny days and seventy-degree temperatures.

My evil plan worked.

SIBLING TIME TOGETHER

Mike was a small youngster. His blond hair, blue eyes, and diminutive size, and the fact that he was a quiet kid, sometimes had others underestimating him.

I didn't.

His mechanical bent showed itself early on. His Tonka trucks were his treasures. He was always breaking them and fixing them, and then building construction sites in our back yard with them.

I firmly believe Mike chose to play the trombone because he found the mechanics of the instrument interesting. It took some convincing from our mom to keep him from taking his apart to figure out how it made the sounds it did.

In Connecticut, we had a hay cutter to mow the front and back lawns and the fields, such as they were. Our older brothers Joe and Moe had gone on to college and beyond, so the job of mowing fell to Mike. I could have driven the huge mower, and unbeknownst to our parents, I already had, but Dad felt the job needed a man's touch. Mike was thirteen. He checked out the mower's engine and its wicked blades, added gas and oil, and drove off. No big deal.

When we were selling our home in CT, our dad went ahead to his new job in Ohio. At the ripe old age of fourteen and a half, Mike became the man of the family. He made sure the house was locked up at night. He fixed each of Sandies "little fender benders" (of which there were many) with little more than "a song and a prayer." We grew used to asking Mike for help with the detritus of our life in rural Connecticut. Even the dogs knew who the new alpha male in town was.

When we finally moved to Ohio, Mike had not only grown in maturity, but also in stature. By his sophomore year in high school, he was six feet, three inches tall. One day he hugged our mom, and, according to our family doctor, "cracked a few of her ribs." Mike was horrified but our mom would hear nothing of either blame or remorse. She told us our PCP had suggested that Mike take up either ballet or Karate to learn how to harness his growing strength.

Initially, Mike thought ballet would be a great idea, figuring there would be lots of girls in the classes, but he settled on karate. Mike continued to study the discipline into adulthood.

A sixth-degree black belt in karate, he teaches self-defense classes for women. When asked why he doesn't charge for the lessons, Mike always says, "Because I have six sisters."

Mike's love for "all things mechanical" has never waned. After college, and gainfully employed in the insurance industry, he still worked on his, (and our) cars. He bought a boat and took us all water skiing, first on the Olentangy River and later on Lake Erie.

Becoming a pilot, and buying a third of a plane came later, much later. By then Mike was married, owned an insurance agency, had a son, and was teaching him, and his friends, karate, also for free.

One thing about my siblings and me: we don't let each other go, no matter how hard some of us tried. In good times and bad, we stick together. This is not to say we don't disagree with each other, loudly, but we still stick. Sometimes Paul, my only-child husband, doesn't get this.

I can say my brother (or sister) is being a jerk, but he can't, ever.

I think having a dad who was an alcoholic bound us in ways only other ACOAs (Adult Children of Alcoholics) can understand. Mike isn't perfect. He can be a pain. He doesn't even share my political affiliations. (Gasp!) But he's my brother, and I love him.

In the fall, we're going, together with our other brother Chris and sister Pat, to our sister Gret's home to help her fix it up. It never occurred to any of us not to do this together.

It's a given. We will argue over where to get takeout, whose turn is it to pay, what the right paint colors are, and who is the best worker.

I can't wait.

MY TRIBE

Every family, every community, every culture, has its rite of passage. I recently learned of a Native American tradition that echoes one of my family's.

In the evening, a young adolescent is led, blindfolded, into the forest. He is told he must remain standing, alone, with the cloth covering his eyes until he can feel the warmth of the sun's rays on his body. The next morning, when he removes the blindfold, he will learn that a member of his tribe has been, unbeknown to him, silently standing guard all night, ready to protect him.

Growing up in a large family is not unlike growing up in a tribe. There is a hierarchy of authority.

There are rules that stem from the serious to the absurd. And there are trials of fire, sometimes on a daily basis.

"Jump! I'll catch you!" (No, he won't.)

"Want to hear the cry of a wounded panther?" (Have your arm twisted until you scream?)

"Try it. You'll like it." (Nope, unless you like Worcestershire sauce in your OJ.)

"Is there a hole in my pants?" (A bad fart-in-the-face joke)

"Let's see if we can get six on a bike." ("Jonnie, you get the rear fender.")

Thanks to my tribe, I learned to avoid confrontation unless I was appreciably larger than my opponent. I became fearless. What could hurt more than being hit with tart green apples thrown with deadly accuracy, or being on the bottom of a seven-kid pig pile, or jumping off the Merritt Parkway Bridge, hoping to land on the grassy median?

Much as my siblings made my life a marathon of snares, ambushes, and disasters to be avoided, much as they were mean, sometimes in Machiavellian ways, there were rules that were followed religiously.

   1. Only members of our family could be the bullies. If a neighborhood kid tried to join in on the pounding going on, he would either be

summarily kicked off or become the next victim.
2. If my sisters were telling me how incredibly ugly my hair, face, or shirt was, their friends, who might have been happy to share their opinions, were not allowed to.
3. When a neighbor "borrowed" my little brother Chris's bike, and returned it with a flat, I, who had just forcibly knocked Chris off the tire swing, walked the bike to the neighbor's house, explained to his parents what had happened, and said it was not necessary that they replace the entire bicycle, that a new tire would suffice.
4. When a girl my little brother Mike adored laughed with her friends at a love note he had written, I walked home with her, retrieved the billet-doux, and made it clear, in a "talk," that she should probably never mess with anyone in my family again.

I think I know what the young Native American boy felt when he removed his blindfold. More than the knowledge that he had been protected, came the realization that he had never been alone, and most probably never would be again.

FAMILY FOOD STORIES

One of the more hazardous events one can witness is dinner time

As mentioned earlier, with a large family, we did not have the option to refuse or complain about the quality or the quantity of our meals. If we did, we were given the option to either go without or go to bed, so my nine siblings and I figured out a barter system that worked fairly often.

I hated asparagus, and Sandie loved it. She hated broccoli, and I didn't mind it. So we swapped whenever we could. I still resent the fact that she moved so far away since many fine restaurants feature asparagus as part of their gourmet fare.

One time, when we were in Germany on a business trip, Paul and I were honored to be served "spargle," the special German version of asparagus. It is planted in mounds. When the tips begin to show, the spargle is cut below the ground, so the spargle is very tender and quite white.

I politely pretended to enjoy it, but I dearly missed having my little sister on my left.

None of the ten of us liked liver. However our dogs loved it. For years our dogs had amazing coats, while we children had many meatless meals on Wednesday nights.

Our big sister, Puss, was often in charge of the rest of us, especially at dinnertime. She concocted a brilliant plan. She would sing the song "Deep in the Heart of Texas" for us. We all loved to sing, especially with Puss, as she could actually sing beautifully.

Puss would begin, in her clear, soprano voice, "The stars at night are big and bright . . ." Then clap four times. When she clapped, we were to take a bite of our dinner. We had to chew quickly because we got to sing the rest of the verse if we finished in time.

"deep in the heart of Texas."

"the prairie sky is wide and high," (clap, clap, clap, clap)

"deep in the heart of Texas."

Our manners were atrocious as we stuffed our faces and chewed openmouthed, but we got to sing, and our dinners were devoured, if not savored.

We were taught how to eat properly and how to behave, and on Sundays, Lady Astor would have been pleased with us, but during the week, it was cowboy and cowgirl time, and we loved sharing our suppers with Puss.

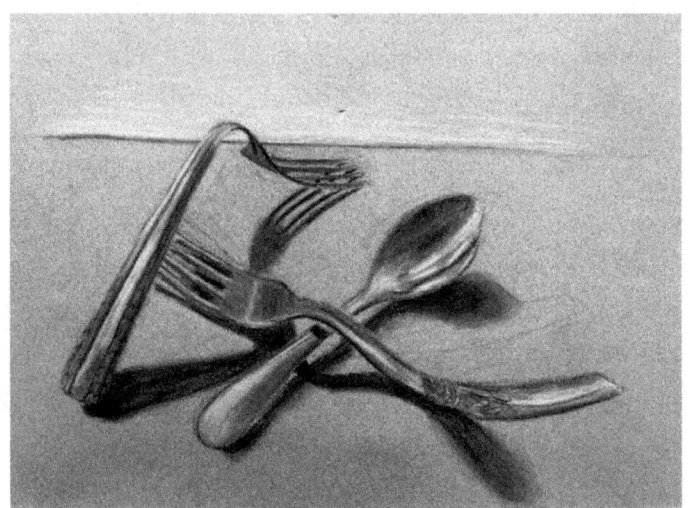

DID THEY REALLY SAY THAT?

When we asked my youngest brother Chris what he wanted to be when he grew up, he said. "I'm going to be a firetruck, with lights and sirens and a spotted dog that loves me."

Impressed by his answer, the rest of us wondered why we had all aimed so much lower than he had.

***

We were playing whiffle ball in the back yard when Ginger tried to steal home.

Joe tripped her and Ginger flew several feet into the air. She landed on home plate but was unable to speak for a few minutes because she had had the wind knocked out of her. Seriously alarmed, Pat and Mike bent close to Ginger's face to try to understand what she was trying to say, between huge gasps for breath…

They weren't sure whether she needed an ambulance or just a drink of water.

Now, up on all fours, with her head hanging down, Ginger finally got out, "I (wheeze) was (huge, gurgling gasp) safe!"

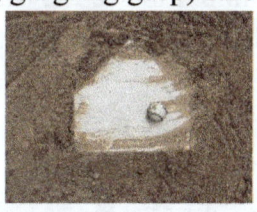

***

While they were visiting, my aunts, my mom's two sisters, got into an argument over the merits of a shower versus a bath. (There was wine involved.) Aggie insisted a shower made one cleaner, whereas Sissy held onto her belief that a bath was just as efficacious. Sissy went to the stairwell, turned back with a dramatic flourish, and said, "I'm going up to take a sponge bath. And when I'm done, you can sniff me all over and we'll see who's right."

***

My great-great-aunt Nell was full of self-importance. Knowing of the many judges, businessmen, and doctors in the family in Lancaster County, Pennsylvania, (the Brubakers, Tuckers, and Allens), she decided to trace the family lineage back a few generations. She got as far as the four Brubaker brothers, who were notorious horse thieves. She then declared, "What matters is not where you come from, but what you make of yourself."

***

My sister Sandie and I were roommates for four years. She was younger than me, but way smarter. I had a journal into which I poured the secrets of my soul. This particular week I had been writing about "boobs" and my painfully obvious lack of them. I was sitting at our desk, my head in my hands, when Sandie peered over my shoulder. Gently, empathetically, she pointed to my sad, sad, journal entry and said, "There's an 'A' in breast."

***

I had taken my grandchildren to see the Mayflower during their spring break from school. I thought my stories about their ancestors had hit home until I overheard this conversation.

Anna: "Let's go upstairs and pretend we're our ansisters."
Alex: "And brothers."

***

There's no hope for any of us.

MY 'SAFE PLACE' IS A TABLE

My "safe place" used to be the fourteen-foot-long dining table we had when we were growing up in rural Connecticut. Its top was a four-inch-thick, solid, single slab of oak. My oldest brother Joe made four, six-foot-long benches for us, his nine siblings, to use. Our dad sat in kingly splendor in a high-backed throne-like chair at the head of the table, our mom at his right.

I folded laundry on it, did my homework on it, played Scrabble with my brothers and sisters on it, ("Snark is SO a word!"), and knelt before it every night in May, (Mary's month), and October, (The Month of the Holy Rosary). We, terrible children that we were, used to try to get whoever was saying his or her section of the rosary to laugh. To do this, we would drop down under the table and poke said person in the belly.

My sister Ginger was very respectful. She would reverently bow her head whenever the name of Jesus was uttered. Unfortunately, when she knelt, she was short, so, she would often bang her chin on the tabletop. When this happened, the rest of us, the savages, would dissolve into giggles.

If you didn't know this fact before this, you do now: My mother was a saint.

On Sundays, the table would be covered with two freshly ironed and starched white damask tablecloths, and then dressed up with my grandmother's sterling and my mom's Haviland Limoges. On those days, our table manners were marginally better, mostly because our mother made the best apple pie in the world. And if we behaved, we were assured a piece.

In the early years of our married lives, none of the ten of us had a house big enough to handle a table that large. Our niece was the first to purchase a mansion, so she got the table.

Twenty years later, I found an old fruitwood door at an estate sale. Nine feet long, three inches thick, and nearly as ugly as my family's oak table, it called to me. So I bought it. Paul, my long-suffering husband, could not believe how much that stupid (his words, not mine) door meant to me, but he made a base for it and it now resides in our dining room.

It has become my new "safe place." I fold laundry on it, play Scrabble on it, do my newspaper homework on it, and write letters to my family on it. We dress it up on Sundays and special occasions. My terrible children's manners are marginally better at those times, because I make the best chocolate cookies in the world, and, if they behave, they are assured a few.

Cracked, chipped, stained and somewhat warped, the door-that-became-a-table seems to have become my children's safe place too.

HOLIDAY CRAZIES

My friends were laughing and talking about their holidays with their crazy relatives.

I asked my siblings if we had any aunts or uncles who did weird stuff. All they came up with was Uncle Bubby, Aunt Sissy, and Moe and Me.

Uncle Bubby could walk on his hands. He used to load his pockets with quarters and then walk around upside down, as we kids scrambled to grab the wealth of coins raining down from his trousers.

Our Aunt Sissy was vain. She never wore her glasses. When she visited us, she always helped out, usually to give Ginger, Gret, and me, our nightly bath. She would scrub Ginger, and then say "Rotate." We would get up, twirl around and then sit down, right back in our original places. Sissy would then wash Ginger again. This worked for years.

Moe and I were bored. Our dad had an amazing Lionel Train set up, but we kids were not allowed to play with it. Dad's holiday train-scape had a snow-covered village whose houses lit up, a depot where the trains were garaged, and signs that read, "DANGER! TRAINS CROSSING!" at all the intersections.

Moe had the brilliant idea to stage a tragic accident on one of the streets that crossed the train tracks. We took five of Moe's small, plastic cars and, with matches, melted them in various places. We then set up an accident with bloody cars stashed atop one another, their sides burnt and smashed in.

We didn't have any pedestrians or drivers, so Moe's army men had to do. They took forever to melt, but we got three reasonably, tragically, injured victims. It was the most fun I ever had with Dad's Lionel Train Village, or with Moe.

None of these stories are about crazy relatives.

They're just about my family being normal.

I wish I had some crazy relatives.

LAISSE FAIRE

My sister-in-law Rita says that our mother's method of rearing us was "laisse faire" to say the least. My brother Chris explains their different philosophies this way.

Rita would say, "I notice a difference in the baby's breathing."

Chris would say, "The baby is breathing. So?"

I think our mother, after giving birth to the first five children, felt that we should keep an eye on each other. And we did.

I will admit sometimes our opinions of what was dangerous, and/or potentially dangerous, were a tad off track.

Most of our summers were spent barefoot in the fields, in the apple trees, or inventing new and different ways to torture each other.

I do know a few of my scars were the direct result of dares I probably should not have taken. The same goes for some of the little kids' physical mementos.

We were fed, clothed, educated, and challenged every day of our lives. Most times by our parents, sometimes by each other.

But we also supported each other when push came to shove, especially when the pushing and shoving was done by someone other than one of us ten.

We still do this now. Support each other. We also still love each other. So maybe laisse faire wasn't such a bad way to parent. At least for our family.

DOLLS I HAVE KNOWN

My friends and I were gabbing the other day about, of all things, the dolls we had as children.

This interested me because I only ever had one, and my brothers and I used her to entice a huge snapping turtle to move toward us. It grabbed my doll's head with its beaky mouth, and smashed her eyes in.

This, to me, made my doll even more cool than it had been. I mean seriously, who else had a doll with a smashed-in face?

I will admit it took me a while to get the turtle to let my brave doll go, but that made the adventure even more exciting. Knowing what I do now about the tensile force a snapping turtle's beaky mouth has, I realize I could have been injured. My poor guardian angel must have been busy keeping me out of danger.

My friends were not amused by my story. They loved their dolls and took great care of them.

They had tea parties and dress-up play. They took them on sleepovers and sometimes to school. Somehow, I don't think my fifth-grade teacher, Sister Rosarita, would have been pleased with my grisly tale of doll and turtle lore.

Sister Rosarita was the nun who told me, "Miss Lane, did I, or did I not tell you that whistling makes the Blessed Mother cry?"

After school, I asked my mom about that and she said, "Jonnie, whistling is a joyful noise. Just don't make that joyful noise in school or near Sister Rosarita." Now, you might think I didn't like Sister Rosarita. But, even at the tender age of ten, I knew how hard she worked to teach us kids. And she let me take three more books out of the library than the other kids could because she knew how much I loved to read. In retrospect, I think maybe if I were reading, I wouldn't be pestering her with the hundreds of great ideas I had to make learning more fun . . .

But I digress. I was talking about dolls. My sisters had dolls. My younger brother Mike had a huge black and white stuffed Panda bear he called 'Teddy.' Teddy was nearly as tall as Mike.

Mike had the same lack of respect for his "doll" that I did because we had a serious trial and convicted Ted of treason. His punishment was to be hanged at sunset. We tied him up by his neck and hung him from the Merritt Parkway Bridge. Some people didn't like seeing that and we had to take him down, but we figured Ted had paid for his crime.

Chris called his stuffed toy dog "Snuffy." Snuffy sometimes wet the bed, and poor innocent Chris was blamed. Snuffy had to go into the washing machine quite often. This bothered Chris so much that he decided to train Snuffy not to do that anymore. (This is one example of how my mom was a genius without saying my mom was a genius.)

I'm guessing my point is, because we mistreated our doll toys, (have that read "had grand adventures with them,") only a few survived.

Seriously? We ten had each other to hug, mistreat, and play with. Who needed dolls?

"I WISH I GREW UP IN THE SAME FAMILY YOU DID."

My brother Mike has said this enough times for me to finally accept that we actually did grow up in different families. I do remember coming home from college and trying to tell our dad that he should ease up on Mike, Pat, and Chris, the three youngest kids in the family. I thought he was being so strict because he was essentially the age of most of our friends' grandparents. That it was a generational thing.

Our dad was an alcoholic. Because of his drinking, he was not a very good father. When he died and we, his ten adult children, returned home for his funeral, our sister Mary Ellen wisely set up a grief session for us. She felt it might ease some of our sorrow and anger.

The psychologist began our meeting with two stipulations:

The first was that we could not talk about anyone who was not present.

The second, which I found way more interesting, was that we could neither interrupt nor contradict another sibling's story. I.E. We couldn't say, "That's not how it happened."

To say those two and a half hours were heartbreaking would be a huge understatement. I had no idea, with the family's move to Ohio, not only how much my dad's drinking had escalated, but also how abusive he had become to Mike, Pat, and Chris.

My life had been cushioned: first because my dad was drinking less when I was around, and, second, because my older siblings protected me. Now, I can see why the "small fries" often have different reactions to the funny stories and memories I share.

I should have been there for them, should have protected them. How did I not see that they needed me?

BROTHERS AREN'T SO BAD

When I was a kid, the term "tomboy" was often used to describe a girl who was athletic or good at sports or one who was not necessarily into dresses. I thought I was a tomboy and was fine with this.

As you may recall, my dad had a regulation baseball field set up on two acres of our family's land. It had limed base paths, a score board, and a huge backstop that kept foul tips from doing damage to any of our neighbors' property or children.

Because of this amazing playground, all ten of us kids grew up playing baseball.

Although my sister Ginger was athletic, she was more into looking pretty and liking boys. These preferences, however, didn't keep her from playing ball with us if we were short a player...

One day a guy called her a tomboy when she stole second. He was playing short and missed the tag. He was embarrassed and sneered at her as she dusted herself off. Ginger wasn't bothered at all by the tomboy crack.

I was.

All of a sudden, the word wasn't as cool as I had thought it was.

Ginger was and still is what some might call a girly girl. She was slender, had blonde, naturally wavy hair and would, more often than not, be found in a skirt or a dress.

Until that day, I hadn't thought being a tomboy was a bad thing. But all of a sudden it was. Was I less of a girl because I liked to run, play ball, and ride bikes?

This wasn't a question for Mom. I needed to talk to a brother. Mom would be all nice and loving. Moe would tell me the truth.

After he told me I was less ugly than I used to be, he said not to worry, that I was a girl, and almost a good one at that. He didn't go crazy with praise, so I believed him. That was when I began to think maybe having brothers wasn't so terrible after all.

MOM'S RING

Nearly a year after my mom died, my dad sent me a letter asking, "Who should get your mother's ring?"

I was a surprised by the question, because as far as I knew Mom's "ring" was two identical, simple silver wedding bands. And why the heck was Dad asking me?

Turns out Dad sent an identical letter to each of my nine siblings. In it he described the ring and told us he did NOT want a barrage of phone calls. He wanted each of us to write down what we thought and why we felt that way. It seems my mom had had a valuable diamond ring, whose stones had once been a part of my great-grandmother's broach. And now our dad wanted us to tell him who should have it.

I pretty much know what each of us wrote to him, because my brother Chris and I were "volunteered" to go through dad's papers after he died. I found all of our letters, bound by a rubber band, in one of his old briefcases.

My oldest brother, Joe, said Dad should sell the ring and set up a college fund for any future grandchildren. My three other brothers thought their six sisters should make the decision. One letter said, "Give it to Jonnie because she is amazing." (Rereading this years later, I realized I probably shouldn't have signed it.)

Five of us six girls felt it should go to Puss, our oldest sister. Simply because she was, and is, the best of us.

After the initial letters arrived, Dad called and offered the ring to three of us kids whom he felt could afford to buy it. His idea being that the other nine would share the monies from the sale.

But then, almost immediately, Dad decided that this might split the family, and changed his mind.

I have to admit it was humbling to read the completely unselfish letters sent by my brothers and sisters to Dad. Not one child felt it should be his. Not one child demanded that it be shared.

Not one child, except for me, took the question lightly.

Dad donated the ring to the Catholic Church, in Columbus, Ohio, in the name of Gretchen Brubaker Lane and her ten children.

WHEN I WAS A CAMEL

I'd love to tell you that my family was unusually creative, but I believe that most of us boomers, who grew up in a pre-computer, pre-cellphone world, were masters in the art of finding unusual and absurd ways to amuse ourselves.

Living on six wooded acres, we ten kids were familiar and comfortable with the wild animals who resided there with us. We often had funerals for the deceased ones we would find. One of our squirrel memorials became legendary when the corpse in question jumped up from his twiggy bier and ran away. He had probably only been stunned by his fall from a taller-than-most tree. Our little sister, Pat, thought he had risen from the dead, "Just like Jeezus."

In the summer, in the back yard we had amazing talent shows. The bed sheets drying on Mom's clothesline were our stage curtains. The boys would have stick-sword battles with gruesome death scenes. Sandie always had to recite something. Her act was not a favorite, mostly because she wrote her own terrible poetry. Gret and Puss did ballet dances they had made up themselves. They were lovely. I was usually a stagehand. I longed to be a star.

One December we performed a Christmas nativity play in our huge walk-in fireplace. Puss got to be Mary because she had the longest hair. Chris got to be Jesus because he was a baby. Mike was a manger cur. "Cur" had been one of his recent spelling/vocabulary words, and he thought Baby Jesus would like dogs, even ones in a bad mood all the time. I wanted to be a "mooing" camel. They told me I couldn't, insisting that "camels don't moo." But what the heck did they know?

I said, "If a camel can nurse her babies like a cow, why can't she moo like a cow too?" I had no idea if a camel could moo, I just wanted a speaking part in the play. And let's face it. A mooing camel might get a few laughs…

I wowed the audience when I gently mooed for baby Jesus. Daddy said I was "a natural." As an actress, my only regret is that at the time I didn't know camels could spit.

I would have been good at that too.

CHRIS'S BIRTHDAY

My brother Chris's kids are planning to roast him on his 70th birthday. They have been asking the rest of us, his siblings, for Chris stories. Betsy, his oldest child thought, at most, we might give her enough material for a page or two of dialogue. Silly person.

Chris is the youngest of ten children. Every single one of us has a plethora of Chris anecdotes.

To be fair to Betsy, Joe was a freshman at Fordham when Chris was born. Puss was a junior in a Catholic girls' academy being heavily pursued by the Sisters of Mercy. Moe was an athletic and academic scholarship freshman at Fairfield Prep, whom we seldom saw.

Going on down the line, the rest of us were, for the most part, way older than Chris, and way more interested in our grammar school lives than in him. So, she was kind of right to think that.

Except for me. I have the greatest knowledge of Chris because for years I actually believed my mom when she punted and said he was mine.

(Said punt involved the seventh birthday party I didn't get because my mom had her tenth baby, ten days before my big day. To make up for my not having a party, Mom handed Chris to me and said he was my special birthday gift.)

Because he had so many older siblings, Chris was more than ready for school when he began.

His vocabulary was excellent. He not only knew multisyllabic words, but he also used them correctly.

When Chris was in first grade, his teacher told him he needed a signed permission slip for an upcoming school trip. Chris got his coat, left school, and walked the mile and a half home to retrieve one. That was the first and only time any of us heard our mom say a bad word, and to a nun!

Having grown up in chaos, Chris was and is unflappable. Bike crashes, rotten apple fights, bunk bed mishaps, and dog chases were all a part of his daily routine.

When he was in eighth grade, Chris wanted to play on his school's football team. However, he was so skinny, he had to be weighed with all of his equipment on, to make the cut.

I wonder if I would remember as much about Chris as I do if I hadn't believed he was mine.

Either way, in telling me what she did, my mom gave him a pit bull of a protective sister.

Nobody messed with him if I was around…except our other siblings.

I thought that was only fair, as they were family.

"ALAS FOR THOSE WHO NEVER SING BUT DIE WITH ALL THEIR MUSIC IN THEM." ~Oliver Wendell Holmes

To each of us is given the gift of song. The melody can be the quiet clacking of a keyboard, the swish of a paint brush, or the soft silence of a ballet slipper. Yet the air is not complete unless it is given voice, harmony, and rhythm through communication with others. Whether "the others" are a crowded newspaper office, a silent tree-shaded bower, or a small freckle-faced admirer, the results are the same… a sonata of self- expression.

"Music" is an allegory for whichever talents we have. I sometimes think those of us who aren't comfortable writing don't realize the myriad avenues available to us to share ourselves and our family's past.

One of my friends is an amazing cook. When she bakes, she tells her children and grandchildren stories about their great-great-grandmother's flight from tyranny. She tells them that when their ancestor had to choose what to bring with her, she took the family recipes, so their culinary history wouldn't be lost.

Another friend was a principal dancer in the ballet. Her story is intricately woven within the corps de ballet. Imagine having to hide the wish to leave one's country because of its corruption. Her story is a sad but inspiring one. And she tells it beautifully in dance.

Not all family histories are tales of good versus evil. Sometimes they are simple tributes to the hardworking, intrepid individuals who came to America for the opportunities it could provide. But their stories should still be told…

We all have music in us. How sad that we might die with our melodies, symphonies, and concerts unheard.

JUST JONNIE

Let me start by saying that no one in my family ever called me "Just Jonnie."

That was a name I gave myself.

I could sing, but Puss who was a lyric soprano, was way better.

I was an athlete, but Moe, who was scouted by professional teams, was better.

I was smart, but Joe and Puss got their MBAs from NYU and Chris got his PHD from Columbia…

I could "cha-cha," but Pat was the most fluid dancer I've ever seen.

I looked nice in a freckled "Howdy Doody-esque" way, but Ginger and Mike, both natural blonds, were actually pretty.

I was musical, but Sandie could play five instruments and memorize entire sonatas while I plunked away on my mandolin.

As we, the remaining seven, have all settled into Senior Citizen Land, I can more easily look at my siblings' gifts with pride instead of envy. More important than any of the special attributes I enumerated is the fact that they are all good people whom I love dearly.

What prompted this unusual introspection, you ask? (With total fascination.)

Well, my brother Chris has had some heart issues, and he recently had a procedure done. My cell has been ringing nonstop with requests for information about it from the others.

"Any news?" and "How's Chris?" have been two recurring queries. Each of my six siblings has a cell phone and the requisite number of digits needed to use said instrument. Somehow, I, "Just Jonnie," have become the "go to" person for family discourse. I'm the one who buys the birthday gifts and then collects the monies for them. I'm the one who reminds the others of special events and anniversaries.

I have no idea when or how this happened, but "Just Jonnie" is okay with the role she is now playing. In fact, she loves it.

PAT'S SHAMPOO

Sophie, our almost two-year-old dog, is an English Cream Golden. Her breed's name is also her color, which is, essentially, off-white, or cream.

For some reason, Sophie prefers her coat to be medium to dark brown. In order to accomplish this, she will jump into or roll in any puddle, swamp, cranberry bog, pond, or river that will accomplish this for her.

She also prefers to smell like nature. Her favorite scents include those of small dead animals, goose leavings, and other dogs' poop. As a result of these charming idiosyncrasies, she is often forced, by me, to take a shower.

Fortunately for me, Paul doesn't seem to mind sharing a twice weekly shower with Miss Sophie. To make this easier, I have "doggy shampoo" in both of our first-floor showers.

My sister Pat, who is a saint, visited last month. Her first morning, she came into the kitchen praising the unique shampoo I had placed in her bathroom…

Pat said she hadn't read the label on the bottle until she got out of the shower and put her glasses on.

"And now," she announced, "I feel like 'SUCH A GOOD GIRL!'"

DOG ADVERTISING.

Our Kids, Practically Perfect

"HAVE YOUR CHILD BRING A SWEATER"

When we moved to upstate New York, Jim was four, Gretchen was almost three, and Steph was two months old. To say the least, somewhat busy, I was a little slow to meet and get to know our neighbors, although they seemed really nice.

Gretchen's third birthday was in October. By that time, Paul had built an amazing gym in our basement, with a balance beam, two swings, a trapeze, and very-low-to-the-ground parallel bars. Jim's side of our full-course basement was Lego Land personified.

I sent Gretchen's birthday party invitations to five of the neighbors' little girls. I planned for the moms to stay for coffee and coffee cake, because that was what I was used to. Moms usually stay when the guests are that young. Or so I thought.

Each mom dropped off her child and left. The atmosphere was, to say the least, chilly. I didn't understand. As the fifth parent was at the door, ready to leave, I asked her. "Won't you please stay for the party? I have tea and coffee and grown-up cake for us."

The mom hesitated and then turned around. Somewhat defiantly, she said, "Around here, we don't tell each other what gifts to bring a birthday child. In fact," she continued, "We all decided we wouldn't spend more than five dollars on any toddler's presents."

Nodding my head in agreement, I congratulated her. "I know," I said. "Three-year-olds don't need anything more than crayons and a coloring book."

She gaped at me. "Then why," she sputtered, "did you write on the invitation, 'Have your child bring a sweater?'"

Now, it was my turn to gape. "Actually," I said, "my plan was to have the party in the basement. and it can be a little cool there this time of the year." I took her downstairs where five cute, would-be gymnasts were swinging on the swings and trying to balance on the balance beam, which was ten inches off the floor.

The neighbor lady looked around the amazing playroom Paul had built for our kids, told me she was going to make some calls, and left. Meanwhile, Gretchen, who had begun to open her gifts, kept saying in a disappointed voice, "Another sweater, another sweater…"

The moms returned, and we all had a good laugh at the mix up. They took back their darling sweaters and Gretchen got two birthday parties that year.

I did not write a special message on her second party invitation. It simply read,

Gretchen's birthday party
October 21, 10:30
at my house.
You know what not to bring.

A KINDERGARTENER AND A FIRST GRADER WALK ONTO A PLAYGROUND

We stood at the schoolyard gate, my kindergartener, first grader, and me.
We watched the kids on the playground with quiet intensity.
Then Gretchen, with a whoop, ran in, and happily began to play.
It was as if she had always been here,
as though this wasn't her first day.
Jim watched a little bit longer, checked the kids, the field, the game
He too then joined the others, but his demeanor wasn't the same
I sighed as I watched, and wondered,
how different could two children be?
I marveled then and I marvel still
at what my towheads were telling me:
That they would live their lives on their own terms,
Gretchen jumping in, saying, "Here I Come!"
Jim would also be a player,
but one who marched to a different drum.
Looking back, I smile, and I marvel at that day,
my children, and me.
The gate to the schoolyard had become something more,
a kind of prophecy.
Jim was playing fiercely now. my athlete, my player,
my star Gretchen smiled, looking back as if to say,
"Don't worry, we won't go far."
Parents now with babes of their own,
I wonder when their kids run free
If their hearts will break a little, too,
because they're a lot like me.

WHEN THE GOING GETS TOUGH, LOWER YOUR STANDARDS

We had a friend named Harry who came up with the weirdest sayings. They were usually both clever and odd and, for some reason, timely. Were the maxims original to him? I have no idea, but he, and his comments, helped me think outside the box, which was usually exactly what I needed at the time.

One of Harry's bon mots was, "When the going gets tough, lower your standards." Initially, I thought this was a joke. But upon closer reflection, I realized it made sense. In times of crisis, we don't need a cleaner house, better meals, or stern lectures. We need all the warmth and comfort a calm loving person can give.

Whenever I was overwhelmed by my family and the challenges we were facing, I would try harder to be all things to all people. I would clean the house, make better meals, and do my volunteer work at night after the kids and Paul were asleep. I would spend hours making the things I could control better.

What I should have been doing was holding the kids, cuddling on the couch with them, and sharing their popcorn and concerns.

Poor Steph was our medical marvel. We discovered she was allergic to shellfish when she was ten. Gretchen saved her life by getting her over to a neighbor's house, who then drove them to the hospital.

Paul took the kids ice skating. He put Steph at the end of a whip line. When she hit her head on the ice, she got a skull fracture.

Jim and Gretchen had their share of injuries too, and I became a regular at our local emergency room.

One time, as one of my favorite ER nurses handed me a cup of tea, I asked her, "Why haven't you guys complained to DYFS about what a terrible mother I am?" She told me they had discussed it, but each time I came in, the injured child was in a different school or sport team's uniform.

When our kids were in their early teens, Paul traveled more often for work. As a consequence, I got pretty good at handling these crises by myself. I learned to tell, fairly quickly, whether the limb in question was broken or sprained...

One time Gretchen went ice skating with our neighbor, Mrs. Orwell, and her kids. When she brought Gretchen home, Mrs. O. told me, "Gretchen fell and hurt her wrist, but since she could move it, I think it's okay."

I thanked Mrs. O. As she drove away, I looked at Gretchen, and asked, "Emergency Room?"

She nodded her head vigorously and off we went. Her wrist was broken.

I now believe when the going gets tough, we should lower our standards.

If one of the kids got injured, pizza – not the best of meals – would be our "feel better" dinner.

If a child came home from school, upset because of a fight with a friend, homework could be left on the back burner, at least for a while. When one of the kids rebelled, instead of punishing him or, more likely, her, immediately, we would have what we called the "stair talk." This involved sitting together on the stairs and listening to each other.

The rules and standards could still be raised, later.

Standards in and of themselves are a good thing. We need their structure. But there is something to be said for lowering them every once in a while.

PAUL'S GOOD REPORT CARD

When our children were young and in grammar school, middle school, and high school, we always celebrated their amazing report cards. We would go to our favorite pizza place, the Reservoir Tavern, and the kids could order anything they wanted.

Were they straight "A" students? Sometimes. And sometimes not. It was just important to Paul and me that we made school and studying and good grades a positive family experience.

When Jim was twelve, Gretchen eleven, and Steph eight, Paul was studying for the CMA Exam (Certified Management Accountant). The course had five tests that had to be passed within a specified amount of time.

The kids would do their homework at the kitchen table, and Paul would do his there too

When Paul got the "report card" saying that he had passed, the children wanted to take their dad out for pizza at the Reservoir.

Jim was in charge. He made it clear to Paul (and me) that this treat was on them. That they were going to use their saved-up allowance money. The girls vigorously nodded their heads in agreement.

When the waitress came to our table, she approached the adults. Paul told her that Jim was in charge, and she went with this beautifully. Jim asked her how much was a pepperoni pizza?

When she told him, he thought for a minute. He then asked her how much would a pizza be that was half pepperoni and half plain? She told him, and again, he calculated.

Then he asked her, "What if we just have pepperoni on two slices?" She took out her calculator, told him the price, and Jim said, "That's what we would like to order.

Jim told Gretchen, Steph, and me that we were having water, but Dad could have a soda, "Whatever kind you want, Dad."

Intrigued by all this byplay, our waitress asked the kids what was the occasion? They beamed and told her, with no little pride, that their dad had passed his tests, and this was his reward for working so hard.

We had a great dinner, and I guess word got around, because the kids got quite a few "Way to Go" pats on their shoulders. Paul even got one.

Jim thanked our waitress and left her a $1.50 tip "Because she did such a great job."

I saw her wiping her eyes.

Mine were a little damp, too.

A MOTHER'S GIFT

Recently, I re-did a bedroom in my house. This in itself is no big deal, as I do this all the time. But my daughter Steph and I swapped a black iron double bed for two black iron twin beds.

Her son, Vince, realized that he wanted his Papa's bed (the double iron one) which he has known, for years, was his gift from his great grandfather I drove to Beverly, and Steph and I moved both bedsteads to their new homes.

I have always loved being a mom-decorator. I took classes and everything.

I purchased new mattress covers and dust ruffles, ironed same, and put together a darling room for Jessie, my granddaughter.

When she visits, Jessie brings her cat, "Sam." Vince, Stephanie, and Casey, are allergic to cats, so, when Jess visits, Sam has to stay downstairs, in the walk-out basement with her.

For a while, I have wanted to make a nicer nest for the two of them.

My "best pal" neighbor is a quilter. She gave me two darling quilts, whose colors were perfect for what I had in mind.

I set up a special room for Jessie and Sam using my neighbor's quilts.

They made the space shine.

Jess's room won't be used often, but when it is, it will be her unique place. As sophisticated as she thinks she is, I know Jessie will be amazed and thrilled by the room and its hand-made pieces.

When I raved about her beautiful work, my "best pal" neighbor, told me, her children are neither interested in, nor appreciative of her pieces.

That doesn't make me sad; it makes me angry. What we do as mothers, wives, and grandmothers is often not appreciated by our progeny. And this is on us.

We've spoiled them. They're used to seeing, having, and wearing the things we have created, with little to no thanks from them.

It's up to us to put a higher value on what we have made. How to do this? I'm not sure.

But, when I give my three kids my latest book, I will ask them to do a review. In order to do this, they will have to read it. Corny, yes, but it's a start.

I will also ask (tell) my husband to give our kids a good swift kick in their nether regions and to remind them how wonderful their mother is . . .

We know we're amazing, but it's time they realize this, too.

If we don't respect ourselves and our talents, neither will they.

HOW TO SPOIL YOUR GRANDCHILDREN

My adult children love to complain about how I spoil their kids...

One of their favorite gripes is that when they were children, I served them their meals and essentially said, "Have at it." There were no special drink requests other than did they want milk or water. And, if they felt they needed something more, they knew how to help themselves.

Now, they say, I'm the grandmother who cuts the crusts off of her grandkids' sandwiches and asks the privileged young diners if they want them cut into triangles or squares.

I'm not quite that bad, but since I have more time now to do special things for my heirs, I like to do them. Being a working mom, a chauffeuring mom, a team mom, a school volunteer mom, a coaching mom, and Paul's wife, did not leave me much time to spoil my children.

Sometimes, (gasp) they even had to make their own school lunches.

***

A side note here. I used to have the kids write their names on their brown paper lunch bags.

Gretchen, who was the only Gretchen in the entire school system, would print, "Gretchen Garstka, second grade, Mr. Connor's Class, Room 5."

Her brother would write, "Jim."

***

I really did think my adult children were exaggerating. But this morning we drove to three stores looking for unflavored water with electrolytes and/or the unflavored electrolyte powder one could add to plain bottled water. Alex, Gretchen's somewhat spoiled youngest, will be playing in a three-day softball tournament in RI, and the temperatures will be in the nineties, again.

I have to admit I began to be a little annoyed when said granddaughter stated she would only drink unflavored electrolyte water. This statement reiterated, after we had driven to a third store in our quest for her holy, unflavored H2O.

The doting, indulgent grandmother in me snapped. I said, "Young Lady, you will drink whatever I buy for you, or you will have plain water, a liquid that has been good enough for everyone on Earth for thousands of years. And if I hear one more word, I will keep the case of bottled water I bought, and just bring a hose attachment so you can drink out of the spigot used by the custodians in the school at the tourney."

Gretchen smiled and said, "Now that's the mother I grew up with."

"THESE ARE THE TIMES THAT TRY MEN'S SOULS." ~ Charles Dickens

This is such a classic quote, one so fitting for this, our times. And, no, I'm not speaking of politics. I'm talking about family holiday gatherings which are a hot bed of problems to be solved and relatives to be placated.

"Whose turn is it to have Christmas, Channukkah, July Fourth, Ground Hog day?"

"Mom, you remember that I am Vegan right?"

"Don't sit Bill next to Grandpa; you know he hates having to listen to his war stories."

Each of our three adult children lives within a fifteen-mile radius of their in-laws.

(Jim's MIL is five houses down on the same street.)

None of them lives any closer than eighty miles from Paul and me.

When they were young marrieds, I stupidly told them, "You will be able to bring great joy or great sorrow to your spouses' families. Bring joy."

Who says such stupid stuff? Worse, whose kids actually listen to advice given them by their mother? Apparently, mine do. Each of them has loved, honored, and cared for their in-laws for years. HOORAY!

Their extended families are good people. But what about Paul and, more important, me?

Other's family traditions have trumped ours. Other's special events have become more important than ours. Other's uncles get to act like idiots at holiday gatherings. What about my brothers?

I've actually grown kind of annoyed that Paul and I are in such good health. Why, you ask?

Because our kids think we don't need them. Because we have good dear friends and lives of our own, they don't think we need to be nurtured or protected or fawned over.

I've come believe that taking the high road stinks. I think it's time for one of us (preferably Paul) to show the need for attention and love. I don't need these because I'm tough. But Paul gets sad. He misses cooking huge, sweet breakfasts for the grandkids. He misses the time spent doing crafts and sports and projects with our children's families.

I guess I might too.

Holidays alone are awful.

DAUGHTERS' DAY

The other day, I was thinking (out loud) about sending our two daughters and our daughter-in-law flowers for Mother's Day. Paul asked me why, or more to the point, "Why now?"

Why? Because after a recent visit from three of our grandkids, two from one family, one from another, both Paul and I commented that they had become really fine young adults. Not to take credit away from the teens themselves, but somewhere along the line, they were taught good manners, how to help out, how to talk to adults, how to offer help, how to clean up after themselves, etc., etc.

None of these behaviors are instinctive. I'm pretty sure it was their mothers who taught them.

I used to think raising our three kids in the seventies, eighties and nineties was somewhat difficult, as societal rules and social mores kept changing so quickly; but in this, the era of computers and cell phones and crazy web sites, a parent's job has become exponentially harder.

How much lead, on their leashes, do we give our puppies?

How can they become responsible adults if we don't give them responsibilities?

How can they become trustworthy if we don't trust them?

Unfortunately, the consequences of a poor decision have become truly insane. If I messed up when growing up, my family, and maybe some neighbors, found out. If my kids messed up when growing up, their friends and classmates might find out. If one of my grandkids messes up, their siblings, their schoolmates, their on-line friends, and possibly the entire East Coast might find out.

Also, if I messed up, people's memory of the event would eventually fade. The same would probably have occurred with my kids' situations.

The internet never forgets. Twenty, thirty, forty years from now, anyone will be able to look up either our grandkids' names or their screwups. And, if they are anything like me, their amazing grandmother, there will be plenty of those.

Back to giving credit where credit is due, our grandkids are amazing, but when they pick up their diplomas, awards, and grants, the words on their lips had better be "Thank you, Mom."

Or they will answer to Grandma Jonnie.

Our Pets – Each One Almost a Purebred

THE VET SAID WHAT?

Since moving here, I have met my share of characters. The ones who stand out however, are the veterinarians. Most of them have been even more homeopathic than I am. And I have been blessed to have their compassionate wisdom. How, you ask can a vet be homeopathic?

Maybe I'm using the wrong word. Some of you may remember Bridget, our Golden Retriever, and the best dog in the whole wide world? When she was eight, she began to have vision issues. I told our vet, and he asked, "So what have you done, in your house, to make things easier for her?"

Surprised, because I'd never had a vet ask stuff like that, I told him I'd taken up all the cool decorative accents around the house that she might trip over or bump into. He said, "And?" I added, "I don't let Paul leave his golf or Pickleball toys around the house anymore." He said, "And?" Now I'm getting a tad peeved.

"And what?" I asked, a little snarkily. He told me that the worst times, in a twenty-four-hour day, for anyone vision impaired, whatever their species, are the dark hours of night. He suggested that we get simple night lights and put them all over the house, that way there would never be a time or place of complete darkness for Bridget.

I was annoyed, but mostly with myself. Why hadn't I thought of this? Paul bought eight simple, square, solar-powered lights and placed them in the halls and rooms in the house less often occupied. The thought being, if we were in a room, there will be lights on. And what a difference! Bridget was a different canine. Additionally, our human house guests loved the security of a lighted path to the bathroom at night, in an unfamiliar house.

The Vet who examined Bridget in her later years (13) told me she had cancer of the tongue. He sat me down and continued. "I could do a biopsy, but I won't do that to a sweetheart her age. I'd have to remove a part of her tongue, and she would be even more miserable than she is now. So here is my prescription. Tonight, call your family members to come say 'goodbye,' and give them no more than a week to do this."

He then scribbled on his prescription pad the following: Monday, give Bridget steak, mashed, Tuesday, salmon mashed, Wednesday chicken mashed, Thursday, lobster, well, you know the drill. Friday, I will come to your house and we will take her pain away."

It's one thing to be a knowledgeable medical professional, whatever ones' specialty. It's another to be this and also be compassionate.

Thank you, Massachusetts veterinarians. Thank you.

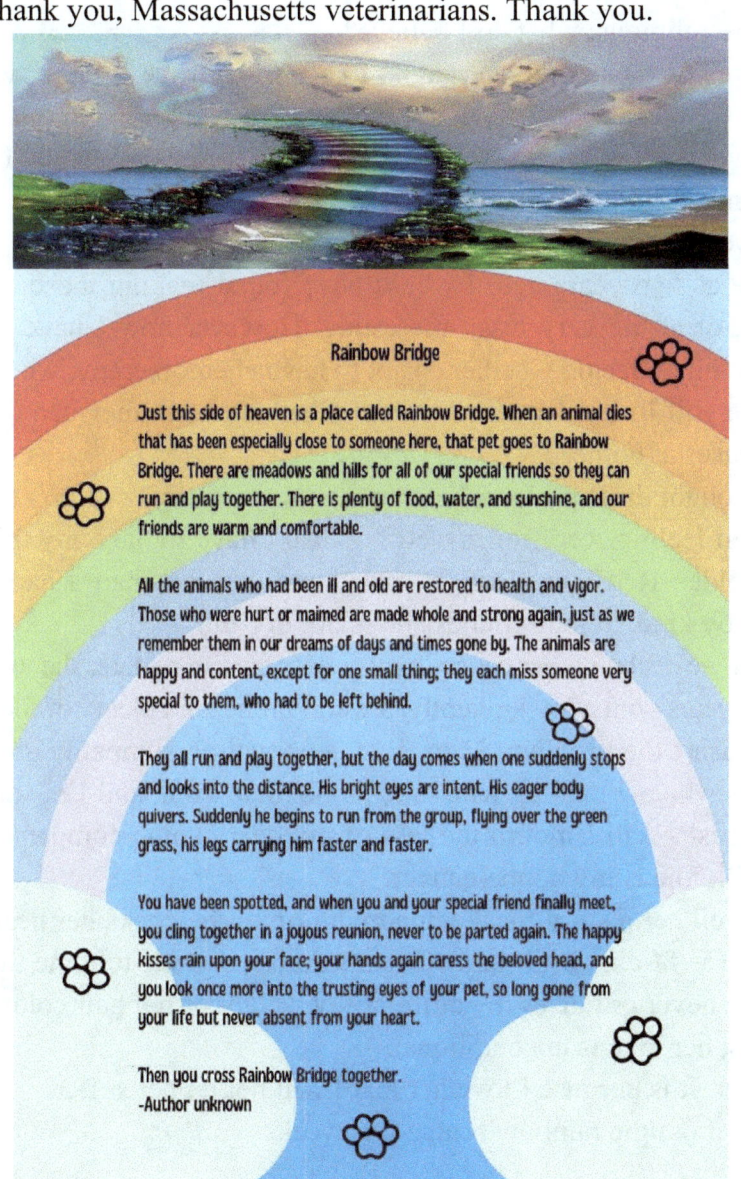

CHOICES

Choices, we all make them.
Some are easy: coffee or tea?
Some are annoying: what's my blankety blank password?
Some are patriotic: what do I stand for?
Some are religious: what do I believe?
Some are personal: who or what do I keep in my life? Who or what do I let go?
Some we face as parents: when do I stand firm? When do I show warmth, compassion?
Some we face as siblings. How much is too much bossiness?
As little as two years ago, I would have found making those choices compelling, or at the very least interesting. However now I have friends who are having to decide whether or not to have chemotherapy, whether or not they can still live independently, and whether or not they can care for their ill spouses at home.
What brought these philosophical thoughts to mind?
I've been feeling sorry for myself because I have to have my thirteen-year-old Golden Retriever, Bridget, put down. She has had a happy life surrounded by kind, human friends and is not in pain.
Whether we deal with her cancer now or at some future date, she will have had thirteen years with a loving family, a warm home, and plenty of food.
Bridget isn't the problem. I am. I've been getting sympathy and hugs from friends who are dealing with much more than I am, and I'm sorry for being so selfish. Will I mourn the loss of my dear canine companion? Of course, I will. She is my doppelganger.
When I tell her a story for the hundredth time, she cocks her head as if to say, "That is fascinating" (and) "I don't think you ever told me that one before." She never criticizes my attire or my weight or my hair color. And, like all dogs, her love is unconditional.
I love her. It is because I love her that I will not let her suffer.
She will cross the rainbow bridge this week.

"DON'T CRY BECAUSE IT'S OVER. SMILE BECAUSE IT HAPPENENED." ~ DR. SEUSS

I haven't been sleeping much since we had to put Bridget, our Golden Retriever, down.

If I were to admit it, I'd say I've been a basket case. The worst time is at night. Trying to keep busy and not think, I washed all the inside windows in the house, laundered each of Bridget's quilts and her bedding, amassed all her medications to donate to the local animal shelter, polished the great room furniture, moved it all around, moved it back, gave myself a facial, began decorating for Christmas, and ironed all the linen napkins I never use.

Keeping busy is how I handle being sad, or angry, or upset.

When Chris's puppy, Jingle Bells, was run over on the Merritt Parkway, I painted his bedroom blue and all his crummy old furniture white, so he wouldn't be sad. It didn't seem to help him, but I felt better.

When Pat broke her arm jumping from her highchair into the Monday pile of laundry, (which might have been my idea), I sewed all her torn stuffed toys and made each of them a new hat.

Paul and I decided to donate some nicer furniture to our vet's "sad room" (our words not his). The thought being, giving Bridget's name to some parts of the room might mitigate our sorrow.

It didn't, but was worth a try.

I'm a mess. Losing my sweet canine has made me question everything. In the early morning hours, I keep asking myself, "Could I have given her another week? Another day? Another hour?" (and) "Does this ever get any easier?"

In some ways, I can almost hear her saying, "You know I will always be with you. Just remember our happy times together."

And I can accept this.

I just need to sleep again.

ANOTHER MEMBER OF THE FAMILY

Last year about this time, I began to lobby to get another pet. Bridget was getting older and slower, and I thought a new furry friend might give her better companionship than her aging humans. So I would leave notes around the house for Paul…

"Roses are red. Violets are blue. Your loving wife wants a puppy, for you."

But then we took care of our daughter Steph's seven-month-old puppy for a few days. Harley, her Golden Doodle, needed a potty run each morning at three AM. So, I reconsidered the puppy idea.

I grew up with cats and decided a cat or a kitten might be a better option. The next sign read:

"Roses are red. Violets are blue. I think we need a kitten or two."

Paul disagreed. He pointed out correctly, logically, that when we wanted to travel another pet would mess with our options. He also mentioned the fact that at this stage of our lives, a dog or cat would probably outlive us. Then where would Sparky or Fluffy go? He was right.

I called our granddaughter Jessie, explained the situation, and asked her if she would consider taking our kitten, Fluffy, when Grandpa and I died. She said, "Of course I would."

I called our daughter Gretchen, explained the situation, and asked her if she would promise to care for our dog, Sparky, when Daddy and I died. She said, "You know I would."

I called our son Jim, explained the situation, and asked him if he would consider taking his father…

SOPHIE BECOMES A WOMAN . . .

Yup, you guessed it. Miss Sophie, our Golden Retriever, is in heat. I've read a ton of articles about this, and I grew up with dogs, so I felt pretty confident I could handle things . . .

I was wrong.

First, even though I knew it was coming, I didn't get the paraphernalia I would need to protect Sophie and our rugs, floors, and furniture. Believe it or not, there are doggy diapers for just this type of situation. Since I didn't have any yet, I used Paul's cotton jersey underwear. I thought it was a pretty good idea. I pushed Sophie's tail through the fly and pulled the rest of the boxers up her doggy waist. When they refused to stay up, I used some old baby diaper pins. When Paul asked me why didn't I use my own underwear? I folded my arms and looked at him.

"Oh," he said. "Yeah."

I should have realized Sophie's time was nearing when she began to roll her eyes whenever I said something. My two daughters began to do the 'eye roll' thing around then, too.

When Gretchen and Steph had their first menses, I took them out of school and we celebrated. We shopped and had lunch and, later on, we got ice cream. None of which would have worked for Sophie.

She had not a clue what was going on, and thought her having to wear Paul's underwear was absurd.

I ordered doggy diapers from Chewy, but Sophie's waist was so small, they fell off all the time.

Our new neighbor, Joe, told me he bought onesies for his small female dog, because her diapers kept falling off, too. The onesies were too small for Miss Sophie, but I found a woman's shirt that had snaps at the crotch. I put a diaper on Soph, then put the shirt on over it. It was ugly, but, as a temporary fix? Not so bad.

Sophie was mortified. So was Paul. He asked, "Do I have to walk her while she is wearing that?" He pointed at the bulky outfit his beautiful dog was wearing.

"Of course not." I reassured him. "She wouldn't be able to use the outdoor facilities with it on, right?"

His sigh of relief was heartfelt.

I also had to let our neighbors, who have dogs, know of Sophie's new harlot-like behavior and the fact that there might be some canine gentlemen callers on our block in the ensuing days...

When I called the breeder and asked her for particulars about the whole process, she cheerfully told me it would all be over in a month. That I just had to walk Sophie, on leash, four times a day, for three more weeks.

Then she could be spayed.

A fun fact? Nowadays, they don't remove a female dog's entire uterus. They just take out her ovaries. This shortens the healing time appreciably.

The "doggy diapers" I ordered for Sophie come in flowered, plaid, and solid-colored options. I couldn't believe Paul actually wanted to weigh in on the decision of which ones to buy. I can't complain about any of this, because I was the one who said we needed a dog.

Of course I love her. Always will. It's just not fun changing diapers again. At least they aren't mine.

Yet.

SOPHIE, THE MUSIC CRITIC

Our puppy Sophie has been acting strange. Normally, the middle section of my truck is her canine condo. She has a quilt, a water dish, and sometimes a few treats stashed in the door's side pockets. She usually settles down and is a calm passenger when we drive around town together.

Lately, however, she has taken to pacing back and forth and whimpering softly.

When I told Paul about this, he asked me if I had changed anything in her doggy domain? I checked the truck's back section and didn't find anything amiss.

However, recently, Hope, my neighbor, gave me some of her husband's old CDs. (My Honda Ridgeline is of 2011 vintage, so it still has a cd player.) The disks were of show tunes, rock n roll, country sounds, and opera. I've been playing them all week, and Sophie didn't seem to mind. She prefers Bon Jovi, John Mellencamp, and The Eagles, but what does she know? She's just a dog.

Yesterday, while I was driving Sophie to doggy daycare, I sang along with Mimi as she performed her aria from *La Boheme*. We made an awesome duet. I harmonized.

Sophie placed a paw on my arm, holding it down, frantically licked the side of my face, and whimpered.

Paul thinks she thought I was dying, as that's the way he views most operatic music.

I, on the other hand, just think she doesn't like opera.

HOW MAX, GRETCHEN'S DOG, TAUGHT ME A LESSON

When we told our daughter, Gretchen, we would watch her dog, Max, for ten days, Paul and I had ulterior motives. Yes, we were happy to have a playmate for our pup Sophie, but we also wanted to help Gretchen's chubby nine-year-old yellow lab to lose some weight. To this end, we began to walk the two dogs, Sophie (fifteen months old) and Max (seven years old), a total of four miles a day.

We also thought we could break Max of the bad habit of sleeping with humans on their bed. I would get into bed at night to read for a while, and Max would jump up to join me. I would push her off and sternly say, "down." She would jump up on the bed again, and I, in a louder voice this time, would say "down" again. Sometimes, this would continue for two more times, before Max would subside, with a sigh, and lie down on her own doggy bed.

I began to pat myself on the back, thinking modestly, I could be a "Dog Whisperer" if I felt like it.

Then Max began to limp, and I realized we might have been pushing her too far, too soon, with the two-mile, twice-a-day, treks.

This became sadly apparent last night, when Max tried to jump up on the bed and fell. She tried again and fell back again. I felt awful. In thinking I could help her drop a few pounds, I had disregarded her age and physical limitations. And now she was hurt...

She didn't weigh much when I lifted her up onto my bed. Not much at all.

A DOGGY VOCABULARY LESSON

Yesterday our puppy Sophie was not feeling well. The reason for this could have been anything from her dining on rabbit and goose poop to her chewing on dirt, sticks, and Paul's socks.

The socks would have done it for me. But I digress.

I sat on the floor with her, rubbed her tummy, and talked in soothing tones. This soon bored me, but she was happy, so I stayed a while. I got to thinking about some of the expressions we humans use that are "canine inspired." As I rubbed and patted Soph, I told her all about them. She seemed fascinated.

Here are a few, although I take exception to some of them:

To rub someone the wrong way
Sniffing around
Barking up the wrong tree
Chasing his tail
Puppy Love
To collar someone
The hair of the dog that bit you
Bitch
Leader of the pack
Sick as a dog
Smells like wet dog
Showing lip
In the doghouse
Licking his wounds

I was on a roll and having fun with my impromptu vocabulary lesson. I looked down at the furry creature I was supposed to be soothing, only to find her asleep and snoring softly.

As some of you may know, I was a middle school English teacher in my former life. Surprisingly, I had that same effect on my human students.

I haven't lost my touch.

My Opinion, Which is Always Right

LET ME TELL YOU A STORY . . .

I have always believed that the best recipes are the ones handed down by family. Why?

Because there is always a back story, and therein lies the tale. We learn about the hardships, the strengths, the humor, the creativity, and the family history that brought about recipes like Aunt Mary's Irish Stew made with Kielbasa, Grandpa's homemade beer that exploded and flooded the cellar, and Mom's potato salad whose ingredient list begins with "take ten pounds of potatoes."

These are our roots. These are the stories that will bind our children, if not with laughter, then with shared embarrassment. Either way, they're learning about their family's beginnings, and that's not bad.

One good example of this theory is my own chocolate chip cookie recipe, which I am sharing here. If you don't mind, please don't tell it to anybody but family.

MY SECRET CHOCOLATE CHIP COOKIE RECIPE

* This recipe is the result of a bad math skill set and early marriage poverty. When I first doubled the recipe on the Nestle's chocolate chip bag, my numbers were off.
** Additionally, when Paul and I got married, I had a limited number of baking utensils, so I had to improvise.
*** Additionally, this is a doubled recipe. If I'm going to make a mess, which I will have to clean up by myself, I might as well produce the most cookies I can.

INGREDIENTS:
- Four eggs
- Four sticks of butter. *Have the butter at room temperature. Melting it in the microwave changes its chemistry. (If my supply of butter is low, I will use margarine, but under protest.)
- Two cups of brown sugar, tamped down
  (In our early years of marriage, I only had liquid measuring cups, so I still use them today.)
- One and a half cups of white granulated sugar
- Two cups of smashed pecans. (I use a meat tenderizer now. Then? A hammer)
- Four and a half cups of flour
- One cup of chocolate chips. Since we, as a family, don't eat a lot of chocolate (because it is bad for the dogs), the amount of chips in our cookies will never be more than two cups. Also, if you (snob) want to use the expensive 80% dark chocolate bars instead of chips, you must smash them with the meat tenderizer/hammer.
- One tablespoon each: salt, baking soda, and vanilla. (In our early years of marriage, I didn't have measuring spoons, so I used a soup spoon. I still do.)

DIRECTIONS:

Once we had kids, I was often "under the gun," so to speak, when making these. (First grade room mother cookies, home and school bake sale, my starving, underprivileged children looking at me with hopeful eyes, etc.) So I just plopped all the ingredients in together. The butter, sugar, and eggs first, then the smashed nuts, then the three soup spoons of stuff, then the flour, with the chips last. (Initially, when I learned about all the little kids with nut allergies, I stopped using pecans. Now, I make half a batch with, and half a batch without, and clearly mark the freezer bags)

Shape the cookie dough into meatball-sized lumps. (This size is the reason for the 13 to 14 minutes of baking time needed.) I usually put only nine meatball-size clumps of dough on a cookie sheet, as the cookies spread while cooking. The finished product should be the size of a small pancake. This makes everyone who says "I only had one cookie" feel righteous.

Bake in a 375-degree preheated oven for 13 to 14 minutes. Turn on the oven light so you can see how your batch is doing. As I, sadly, learned, cookies continue to cook after their removal from the oven, so too dark in the oven, will be too well done in the tummy.

Cool the cookies for three to five minutes. Then remove them from the cookie sheet.

After they have cooled, I freeze each batch. This keeps marauding children, dogs, and husbands from eating up the works.

SOME HINTS:

It is perfectly okay for your "helpers" to lick the beaters and/or sample the chocolate chips. (Salmonella? Oh please! As if a teaspoon of raw dough will kill the child who finished the dog's food when Taffy left a few morsels in her dish.)

It is also okay for you to break a few of the cookies in the first batch, then pretend they won't be good enough for the PTA Bake Sale. You can then, reluctantly, hesitantly, ask the kids if they would mind eating some of the "broken ones."

****

I know each and every one of us has a family food tale. Whether it was a disaster or a triumph, whether it started a fire or a flood (set the sprinklers off), whether it was hated (liver) or illegal (marijuana brownies), there is a story that needs to be told. Your children should know their great-grandmother was a "bad ass." It won't hurt them to know others in their family had problems and messed up. Being perfect is not only impossible, it's also boring. Tell your kids. Tell them.

A NEW FOURTH OF JULY TRADITION

The fourth of July has become a sort of mixed bag of a holiday. While it honors our country's independence, those who helped us achieve and maintain it often have a problem with the way we choose to celebrate it.

Fireworks and firecrackers and their attending flashing lights and loud bangs can be triggers to those who suffer from PTSD, especially our military family members. (Post-Traumatic Stress Disorder is a mental and behavior disorder that can develop because of exposure to a traumatic event, such as sexual assault, warfare, child abuse, domestic violence, or other threats to a person's life.)

It seems to me; lighted candles and patriotic songs and stories can just as beautifully honor how far we have come as a country as fireworks can.

More, a respectful silence can speak just as loudly, perhaps even louder, to the gratitude and empathy we have for those who have served us so well.

Our saying "Thank you for your service" and then ignoring the trauma our soldiers experienced while serving, seems counter intuitive.

Maybe next year, we could leave Tchaikovsky's *1812 Overture* in the concert hall.

Maybe we could light a thousand candles, and maybe we could show our children that while sometimes war is necessary, its consequences last far beyond its glorious end.

ANGELS AMONG US

Trying to keep track of my grandkids, I have been checking out all sorts of social media. Last week I found out about something I felt compelled to share. It is called either an "angel shot" or an "angel drink."

An "angel shot" is not a vaccine. It's a code word. Women can use it if they need help. It is believed the idea originally came from England. A woman at a bar, or club, or concert, or a sporting event, could ask if "Angela" is around. The barkeep immediately realizes the individual is in trouble and goes into a routine already set up to help.

In America, the idea is catching on. Of course, we put a Yankee spin on it. An "Angel Shot" can have accessories. An angel shot "with lime" means call the police. An angel shot "neat" means I need someone to escort me to my car. And an angel "with ice" means please call me a taxi or an Uber.

I sent this information to each of my three children, and to our three oldest grandchildren. Will gave me the eye roll look, but I reminded him that he, a guy, could also be in trouble, that he could have college friends, guys or girls, who might need help, and that it was important that he know the drill.

I know, I know not all young adults are bar hoppers or club aficionados, but there will be bridesmaids' celebrations and bachelor parties, and those attending them won't be drinking lemonade.

A friend asked me, "If you write about this, won't it defeat the purpose of the word phrase being a code?" To some extent, she is right. But this message needs to get out there, and I'm pretty sure the type of person who would drug or use force on another is not your typical reader of my work.

I write about my job as a wife, a mother, and a grandmother. One of the more important aspects of this, is to teach and protect those I love.

As you might know, I sometimes use humor to remind people not to mess with my family. But if you are my friend, then your family is my family. And I'm worried about them too.

"COWARDS DIE MANY TIMES. THE VALIANT TASTE OF DEATH BUT ONCE." ~*Julius Caesar*, Shakespeare

Women for Trump?
When he has no respect for women or his three wives. When twenty-five women have accused him of sexual assault. When he mocks us and brags about his ability to fondle us whenever he wants? How could any woman support this man?

Veterans for Trump?
When he calls them names and mocks their love of country. When two of my brothers are suffering because of their service. When Trump intervened in military justice and pardoned a man convicted of war crimes. How could any veteran support this man?

Catholics for Trump?
When he, the classic and smug example of every cardinal sin is embraced by the Catholic Church and the "Religious Right." How could any Catholic support this man?

Children for Trump?
How special that their parents are teaching them, through their example, that lying, cheating, being a traitor, and disrespecting women is okay. That grandma and grandpa are expendable. That science doesn't matter, that people of color are bad. How could any person, child or adult, support this man?

Republicans for Trump?
When they see how he is destroying the Republican Party and all that it used to represent, how could any Republicans support this man?

Being a coward has become the norm in my country.

Looking the other way has become the norm for my country.

Last year my family and I visited Canada. When asked, I actually wanted to lie and say I wasn't an American.

How special was that?

TO BELIEVE OR NOT TO BELIEVE, THAT IS THE QUESTION

Paul and I attended another graduation this past weekend. This one was a high school graduation in southern New Jersey. The five-and-a-half-hour drive gave us plenty of time to discuss a million things. After we had exhausted all the important topics (grandkids, our adult children, lunch, vacation plans, getting another dog), we ventured into politics and religion.

Years ago, I left the Catholic Church. I very nobly thought, "This is my faith journey, I will not interfere with Paul's." And so far, this has worked. I took the same stance with my children and grandchildren's religious paths. I think the example my devout Catholic mother gave the ten of us, her children, pointed me in this direction.

Joe converted to the Episcopalian Faith. Mike and Moe felt Buddhism was the path for them. Moe stuck with the rosary, saying "Prayer beads are prayer beads." Puss chose Congregationalism. Ginger and Sandie atheism. Chris and Gret remained Roman Catholic. Pat and I became what we called "cafeteria Catholics" since we pick and choose which tenets of the Catholic Church we will follow, rather like kids in a school lunchroom.

The Roe V Wade decision has me rethinking whether or not I can accept Paul's decision to remain and support a church that is antithetical to everything I believe in. With honest concern, Paul asked me why I was so angry with the Church? I think part of it is and has been a sense of betrayal. For forty-five years I blindly believed everything I was taught, and I taught children the same pap.

I believe it was the last confirmation course I taught that opened my eyes. The Church was saying that rapes were only three percent of the reasons for abortions. That the rest were because of selfish and murderous desires to have more of everything but love, generosity, and faith. This was too skewed and erroneous a pill even for me to swallow.

I began to tell my students that in the eyes of the Church, receiving the sacrament of Confirmation made them adults. To me, this meant they should use the brains and the education they have been given to chart their own courses. I told them to question everything. Study other faiths. Read. Read some more. That blind faith is just that: "blind." This message led to some amazing discussions. I learned more from those bright children than they ever learned from me.

As for me, it was a beginning of a different sort. I now knew that being so active in the RC church, with three sisters who were nuns, having studied under Jesuits, had shown me where all the bodies were buried. It also showed me why I got so upset. To answer Paul's question. I'm upset because I'm ashamed of my former Church and of myself.

Paul still goes to Mass. He still supports the Catholic Church. It bothers me. But fifty-five years of marriage have shown me that he is a good and decent man, and an amazing husband and father. I don't think he should quit the Church because of me. But I wouldn't mind if he did.

AN IMPORTANT LETTER TO MY FAMILY

Dear Everyone in my family, boys and girls, young men and young women, older men, and older women,

Today I have committed to march for a woman's right to her own body. I feel stupid and old and uncomfortable, but I have to do this. How can I tell you to stand up for what you believe, if I don't?

Whether or not you believe in abortion, we, the people, must keep it a right, for women everywhere.

One of the premises on which our country was founded was the separation of church and state. Someone else's belief should never be imposed on you. Nor should you ever impose your beliefs on others.

Losing this basic right, the autonomy of all of our bodies, male and female, can and should never be taken lightly.

I promise you this Supreme Court disaster will only be the beginning.

I'm writing this to explain why I am protesting for something the Catholic Church has told us is wrong. Sadly, priests, bishops, and cardinals are not men of medicine. Nor should they be involved in this political takeover of women's choices for their bodies, their lives, and their futures.

I've only made one sign to carry. It says:

> HOW CAN I TELL MY GRANDCHILDREN TO
> STAND UP FOR THEIR RIGHTS, IF I DON'T STAND
> WITH THEM?

Dear Ones,

Those of you old enough to vote. Vote.

If you don't, then you will only have yourselves to blame for a dystopian future for yourselves and your children.

Love,

Jonnie, Mom, Grandma

I REMEMBER MARJI

My husband Paul enjoyed making things. His current project was to build a stone wall that would wrap around the back half acre of our property. On weekends, he and I would scour the local woods for stones the size and shape he wanted.

I had an amazing idea. (I often get them.) I would get Kenny, a neighbor's son, who was working construction that summer, to find and deliver a half yard (truck load) of rocks as a surprise birthday present for Paul. Paul was going to LOVE it!

Ken refused my offer of money, so we decided I would pay him with chocolate chip cookies every weekend for the rest of the summer (10 weeks).

My brilliant plan included me placing one beautifully wrapped rock alongside Paul's other birthday gifts, He was going to be really, really happy.

IN ILLO TEMPUS CONCEPTUS BONUS ERAT. (It seemed like a good idea at the time)

Kenny came through. However, he dropped the half yard of rocks on the side driveway, in front of the four-foot-high stone wall there. If I didn't move the stones before Paul came home from work, his birthday surprise would be ruined.

I ran into the family room and asked my three kids to help. When they heard what was involved, they said, "No way." According to them, I always had crazy ideas, like this one, and, they always had to rescue me.

Since they were right, I went back outside and began lifting rocks and throwing them over the wall. I convinced myself I would be able to get them all safely hidden from view in the three hours before Paul got home.

I felt a presence beside me, and it was my across-the-street-neighbor, Marji. Without a word, she began to help me. We were about twenty rocks in when Jim, Gretchen, and Steph, in abashed silence, joined us.

Seeing Marji, who was "really" old, at least sixty, helping me, had made the kids ashamed of themselves. We all finished the job long before Paul got home.

That was the quintessential Marji. She never preached; she just led by example. I loved her very much, and I miss her every day.

Especially when I get a great idea.

FUNERAL STORIES

It is a sad fact that at this stage of our lives, Paul and I will attend more life celebrations than graduations, weddings, or religious ceremonies combined. Last summer was a case in point.

Paul wanted me to go with him to a memorial for a guy he knew from golf. I didn't know him, but that was okay, because I don't have to know everybody Paul knows.

On the way to the service, I asked Paul about his friend. Paul said he had only met the guy once.

Intrigued, I must have given him my "this is unusual" look, because he continued, somewhat defensively, "Bill only moved here six months ago, and probably didn't know many people. We're doing this for his family."

It was a loving, albeit brief event. What was sad though was how few men stood up to reminisce and tell tall tales about Bill and his prowess, or lack thereof, on the golf course. There were no stories detailing idiotic college mishaps or laughing work-related bombs. There was no personal humor to act as a buffer for the sorrow the family must have felt.

I kept elbowing Paul and hissing, "Get up! Say something!" But he didn't. He felt unprepared.

On the way home, we discussed how sad and lonely the afternoon had felt. We also discussed the guilt we both felt that we had somehow let Bill and his family down.

Since then, Paul and I have decided to never again go to a memorial, life celebration, or funeral unarmed, so to speak. Weddings and births are happy occasions, and clever, funny stories seem to rise out of thin air. Funeral laughs not so much.

What this decision has done is given us the motivation to reminisce about the individual being remembered. Of course, we begin with sadness initially, but then we remind each other there were good times in a life well lived.

www.ingramcontent.com/pod-product-compliance
Lightning Source LLC
LaVergne TN
LVHW021714080426
835510LV00010B/987